A DEFOE COMPANION

A Defoe Companion

J. R. Hammond

Barnes & Noble Books

First published in Great Britain 1993 by
THE MACMILLAN PRESS LTD
Houndmills, Basingstoke, Hampshire RG21 2XS
and London
Companies and representatives
throughout the world

This book is published in Macmillan's *Literary Companions* series

A catalogue record for this book is available
from the British Library.

ISBN 0–333–51328–2

Printed in Hong Kong

First published in the United States of America 1993 by
BARNES & NOBLE BOOKS
4720 Boston Way
Lanham, MD 20706

Library of Congress Cataloging-in-Publication Data
Hammond, J. R. (John R.), 1933–
A Defoe companion / J. R. Hammond.
p.   cm.
Includes bibliographical references and index.
ISBN 0–389–21006–4
1. Defoe, Daniel, 1661?–1731—Handbooks, manuals, etc.   I. Title.
PR3407.H35   1993
823'.6—dc20
                                        92–39387
                                        CIP

Hail to thee, spirit of Defoe! What does not my own poor self owe to thee! England has better bards than either Greece or Rome, yet I could spare them easier far than Defoe.

George Borrow, *Lavengro*

Contents

List of Plates

For the provision of illustrations, and permission to reproduce them, grateful acknowledgements are made to: Hulton Picture Company (1); British Library (2, 3, 5); Kenneth Monkman (4); Welcome Institute Library, London (6).

Preface

Daniel Defoe occupies a central place in the history of English literature. As the author of *Robinson Crusoe* and *Moll Flanders* he can claim with some justification to be the first English novelist and the father of the novel as we know it today. He was one of the earliest practitioners of the 'desert island' myth which has proved to be such a seminal influence on the human imagination. In *A Journal of the Plague Year* and *A Tour through the Whole Island of Great Britain* he forged a distinctive documentary style which deeply influenced later writers, including Poe, Stevenson, Wells and Orwell.

This *Companion* aims to present Defoe afresh and to reappraise him from a late twentieth-century standpoint. An introductory chapter presents an overview of his life and times, tracing the forces which shaped him as man and writer. This is followed by a summary of his literary achievement, discussing in particular his pioneering approach to the novel and his strengths and weaknesses as a novelist of character. Each of the principal works is then examined in detail and placed in its literary and biographical context. The *Companion* also contains a dictionary of the characters and places that have a significant role in the novels, and a checklist of the film versions based on Defoe's works. In summarising his life and achievement and offering a critical overview of his contribution to the development of the novel the *Companion* seeks to re-establish Defoe as a pivotal figure in the history of literature.

I would like to acknowledge my indebtedness to a number of critical works which preceded mine, in particular to James Sutherland's excellent biography of Defoe, first published in 1937 and still unsuperseded, and his stimulating *Daniel Defoe: A Critical Study*. Pat Rogers's works have also been indispensable, especially his volume on Defoe in the *Critical Heritage* series and his admirable edition of the *Tour* with its full scholarly apparatus. Details of these and other relevant works will be found in the bibliography.

My friend and historian Dr Michael Honeybone has read the draft of the opening chapter and commented helpfully upon it. Norman Page, Professor of Modern English Literature at the University of Nottingham, has been helpful and encouraging as always. I also wish to place on record my thanks to the staff of the following libraries: British Library, London; University of Nottingham Library; National Newspaper Library, Colindale; Stoke Newington District Library (London Borough of Hackney). Finally I would like to record my warm appreciation to Joy Bremer for typing the manuscript with such care, and to my wife for her unfailing patience and understanding during the throes of composition.

J. R. HAMMOND

Author's Note

The text used for the extracts from Defoe's fiction is that of the World's Classics edition, published by Oxford University Press. Page references in these chapters are to this edition.

Page references in the chapter on *A Tour through the Whole Island of Great Britain* are to the Penguin Classics edition.

Publication details of these editions are given in the Bibliography.

Part I

The Making of a Novelist

The world into which Daniel Defoe was born was one on a much smaller scale than our own. England was a rural landscape composed of a very large number of small settlements; three-quarters of the population lived in villages. The largest city, London, had a population of half a million, nearly 10 per cent of the country as a whole. The average size of an English town was a little over 1000 people. It was a pre-industrial world, one in which there were no machines, no daily newspapers, and no rapid means of communication. It was a *localised* world, in which the dominant means of transport was horseback. As Peter Laslett expresses the situation in *The World We Have Lost*: 'Before the coming of the bicycle and the paved highway, there was a fixed distance from the labourer's cottage beyond which a full day's work was out of the question – it took too long to get there and back'.[1] It is difficult for us at the end of the twentieth century, living in a sophisticated technological age, to make the imaginative leap necessary to contemplate this minuscule, localised world. By comparison with our own, it would seem a world at a much slower pace, in which distances were measured in days rather than hours.

But it should not be inferred from this that the seventeenth-century world was a static one. Civil strife was commonplace in England and on the continent of Europe. From 1642 to 1649 England was embroiled in a civil war between Puritans (supporters of parliamentary government) and Royalists (supporters of the monarchy and the divine right of kings). The two civil wars were followed by Cromwell's protectorate and a long period of political instability. It was a time of fierce argument between rival parties and factions, for the English were bitterly divided over a range of political and religious issues. Fundamental to these disagreements was the argument over what should be the relationship between Crown and Parliament. This debate was raging intermittently throughout Defoe's early life and was not resolved until the 'Glorious Revolution' of 1688, by which time he was 28. These decades of conflict in which England was divided against itself help to explain the polemical nature of much of his early writing and the restlessness which is so characteristic of his work.

Daniel Defoe was born in London in the autumn of 1660. His exact date of birth is not known, since no written record of his birth or baptism has survived.[2] He was the son of James and Alice Foe of the parish of St Giles Cripplegate, lying just beyond the wall on the northern edge of the City of London (his real name was Foe, but for convenience he will be referred to as Defoe throughout this book). James Foe was a tallow chandler – a dealer in candles and soap – and later became a merchant of some substance, extending his activities into overseas trade. He was the son of a Northamptonshire yeoman and was a sober and earnest Puritan, or Dissenter as they were termed at that time. Little or nothing is known of Alice Foe – not even her maiden surname is recorded – and biographers are hard put to it to explain how the couple came to rear such a remarkable son. There is no evidence of any literary or creative background in Defoe's ancestry, though the values inculcated in his childhood home were those he remembered all his life.

He was brought up in a world in which the predominant values were orderliness, discipline, self-sufficiency and respectability; to improve one's lot through one's own industry was the prevailing ethic. As a boy Defoe must have been familiar with such terms as 'merchant', 'trade' and 'commerce' and been impressed by the knowledge that his father had attained a position of modest prosperity as a result of hard work and initiative. Some indication of the earnestness of his childhood background can be gleaned from the fact that as a boy he wrote out in longhand the whole of the first five books of the Old Testament.

Daniel had two older sisters, Mary (born 1657) and Elizabeth (born in 1659), but the latter died in infancy. His boyhood home was situated in Swan Alley in the parish of St Stephen, Coleman Street, within walking distance of St Paul's Cathedral and the Royal Exchange. The house was apparently one of a series opening on to a courtyard; in the courtyard stood several sheds where James Foe stored his wares. The atmosphere was quiet and respectable, but just beyond the courtyard lay the bustle of the City and the narrow festering alleys leading down to the Thames.

When Daniel was still a small boy his life was riven by two events which haunted his imagination for many years to come: the Plague and the Fire of London. Periodic outbreaks of bubonic plague were accepted by many in London as a fact of life, but the outbreak which reached the City during the early months of 1665 was particularly virulent. Soon the weekly bills of mortality were reaching appalling levels; a weekly figure of 500 or more deaths in the parish of St Giles alone was by no means uncommon. The King and his court withdrew to Oxford, and many merchants fled with their wives and families into the country. Defoe can have had few personal memories of the Plague itself, for the evidence suggests that the family moved to Buckinghamshire for the duration of the epidemic, but it made a deep impact upon him: it must have been a topic of conversation in the Foe household for years afterwards, especially in a religious family where such outbreaks were regarded as acts of God and punishments for sinful behaviour. He retained a vivid memory of deserted streets that had once been populous, of grass growing among the cobblestones, of the crying of the bereaved. Three years after the plague had ceased, when Defoe was a boy of nine, building work in Bishopsgate Street exposed the site of one of the pits in which bodies of the victims had been buried. The sight of the victims, some still bearing their hair, made a deep impression on the mind of an imaginative child. Years later he was able to weave this memory into his masterly *Journal of the Plague Year*, a distillation of all he had read and been told concerning the terrible epidemic.

London had barely recovered from the plague when it was overtaken by the Great Fire which raged for four days and nights, destroying St Paul's and 87 parish churches, including St Stephen, and 13,000 houses. Many of the familiar landmarks Defoe had seen as a boy were gutted, including the Royal Exchange, the Customs House and the Guildhall. He never forgot the impression this disaster made upon him, and years afterwards wrote:

> I remember very well what I saw with a sad heart, though I was but young; I mean the Fire of London. That all endeavours having been fruitlessly used to abate the fire, the people gave it over, and despairing citizens looked on and saw the devastation of their dwellings with a kind of stupidity caused by amazement.[3]

This disaster, following so quickly on the heels of the plague, remained in Daniel's memory for the remainder of his life. Though the Foe household and shop escaped destruction in the fire many of James Foe's friends and business associates were directly affected by it. Daniel could not forget the sight of the sky glowing at night, the smoking ruins of the City, and the homeless camping on the grass.

An important consequence of the fire was that the City had to be rebuilt, which meant that the area of London he knew best was *modern* rather than antiquated. In place of tumbledown buildings of timber and thatch grew a whole new London of brick and stone. This is of more than symbolic significance, for all his life Defoe was associated with the idea of modernity: with the notion that man must make a systematic effort to improve his lot. (It is interesting to note that H. G. Wells's parents, Joseph and Sarah Wells, were married in 1853 in the rebuilt parish church of St Stephen, Coleman Street: a strange coincidence when one reflects that Defoe was one of Wells's literary mentors and that the two writers had much in common.)

When Defoe was 11 his father decided to send him to a boarding school at Dorking in Surrey, where he remained for five years (1671–6). The school was kept by the Reverend James Fisher, an elderly nonconformist clergyman and a former Cambridge scholar. Fisher had a passionate faith in the virtues of a classical education, and instilled into his pupils a knowledge of Latin and Greek. Latin made a strong impact on young Daniel: all his life he kept Latin books in his library, and was fond of embellishing his pamphlets and essays with Latin texts. Much time was spent on English grammar and the minutiae of parsing and construing. Defoe does not record any reminiscences of his schooling, though he retained affectionate memories of Dorking and its surrounding scenery. These were highly impressionable years and he took a lively interest in politics from an early age. He must have been aware of the national and international events that were happening around him and talked about at home and at school: the war between England and Holland; the freezing of the assets of the Lombard Street banks by Charles II (which caused the ruin of many businessmen); the uneasy truce between the Crown and the Dissenters; the rise to fame of the young William of Orange.

In 1676, soon after his sixteenth birthday, he was sent by his father to the dissenting academy kept by the Reverend Charles Morton at Newington Green, Stoke Newington. James Foe intended to enter his son for the ministry and felt that three years at Morton's Academy would be an excellent training for this. This was a remarkable school, and though Defoe never entered the ministry – and therefore deeply disappointed his father – he had reason to be grateful for such a fine opportunity. Under Morton's guidance he studied logic, politics, English, philosophy and mathematics, and continued his instruction in Latin and Greek. Morton seems to have been a teacher of considerable ability who, unusually for his time, expressed himself in plain, concise English and did his utmost to inculcate in his pupils the facility of writing in a fluent, unaffected style. Defoe's debt to him was incalculable. Not only was he deeply influenced by Morton as a teacher but under his stimulus he was reading widely outside the curriculum, including travel, history, poetry (especially Samuel Butler's *Hudibras*) and devotional literature. It is difficult to exaggerate the importance of these years at Newington Green on the eager and curious Defoe. He imbibed from Morton much more than a thorough academic grounding in the classics: he derived an enquiring attitude of mind, an insight into science, and a love of the English language which never left him. Above all he acquired the ability to write in a persuasive, flexible style that followed the natural rhythms of conversation.

Morton was an erudite man but by no means a dry pedant. He encouraged his pupils to think for themselves and placed much stress on the need for individual reading and enquiry. These were years of intellectual ferment when there was widespread discussion of politics and religion. Bunyan's *Pilgrims Progress* was published in 1678– eagerly read by Defoe as soon as it appeared – and Defoe was also reading with admiration the poetry of Andrew Marvell, the Earl of Rochester and John Milton. Inspired by these writings, he tried his hand at composing a volume of poetry, *Meditations*, but this reveals little indication of literary promise. He was still a young man feeling his way in the world and as yet uncertain which profession he wished to follow. Towards the end of 1679 he reached one of the crucial decisions of his life and rejected the idea of becoming a dissenting minister. Whether this decision was taken on theological grounds is not known, but clearly he felt he would be a misfit as a clergyman and cast about for some other means of earning his livelihood.

The 1680s were a promising time for an energetic young man to establish himself as a tradesman. Though it was still a pre-industrial society, the outlines of the modern business world were already in place. These years saw a rapid expansion in the number of joint stock companies, company promoters, and dealers in stocks and shares. A penny post was inaugurated in 1680 and this made possible several postal deliveries in the London area each day. Banking and insurance systems were becoming increasingly well established, and there was a considerable growth of overseas trade. Above all it was a time of business confidence when a spirit of optimism was abroad. Filled with the ambition and self-confidence of youth, Defoe set himself up as a London merchant, trading in hosiery, wines and spirits, tobacco and other commodities. He continued in this capacity from 1680 to 1692: years of decisive importance to his personal development and the shaping of his world. It was the custom then and for many years afterwards for a young man who wished to pursue a career as a businessman to be apprenticed to a tradesman for seven years before setting up on his own. Defoe bypassed this convention, establishing himself as a dealer and wholesaler at the age of twenty, presumably with the aid of money provided by his father. This must have led to some resentment from his fellow businessmen who had had to learn 'the hard way'. It also meant that he launched his venture with great enthusiasm but a lack of practical experience. His undoubted energy and resilience carried him forward for some years, but his inexperience proved in the long term to be his undoing.

Defoe began to travel widely in the course of his business, journeying on horseback to many parts of England and Scotland, and developing a taste for solitary travel which remained with him throughout his life. Not only did he become well acquainted with his native land, making personal contacts with manufacturers, but he also travelled extensively in Europe, especially Spain and France. 'A true-bred merchant ... understands languages without books', he wrote, 'geography without maps, his journals and trading-voyages delineate the world.'[4]

On 1 January 1684 he married Mary Tuffley, the only daughter of a prosperous dissenting merchant. Years later, when he came to write his *Complete English Tradesman*, he entitled one of his chapters 'Of a Tradesman's Marrying Too Soon' and strongly counselled against early marriage, arguing that tradesmen should not involve themselves in the expense of a family 'before they were in a way of gaining sufficient to support it'. Clearly, he had rejected his own advice for he was 23 and Mary was 20. She brought him a dowry of £3700, a very considerable sum for those days. She proved to be a loyal and patient wife, bearing him eight children (of whom two died in infancy) and holding the family together through all the vagaries of his career and his frequent absences from home. Shortly after his marriage he established himself in substantial premises in Freeman's Yard, on the north side of Cornhill, then a high-class area newly rebuilt after the Fire.

In 1688 an event occurred of national importance which profoundly affected his life and outlook. On 5 November of that year the forces of William of Orange landed at Torbay; an invasion swiftly followed by the collapse of James II and his regime. This heralded what became known as 'The Glorious Revolution', the end of the divine right of kings and the establishment once and for all of the supremacy of Parliament. Defoe was an enthusiastic supporter of the Revolution and of all it embodied: the assertion of the fundamental rights of Parliament; the limitation of the royal prerogative; and legal toleration for protestant dissenters. From now until William's death Defoe was an unstinting admirer of the new King and sought every opportunity to serve him. To Defoe, a dissenter and a firm champion of the people, the Revolution marked the end of years of uncertainty and finally settled the relationship between Crown and Parliament. H. G. Wells expressed this sense of finality in these terms:

> There have been no revolutions, no deliberate restatements or abandonments of opinion in England since the days of the fine gentry, since 1688 or thereabouts ... there have been changes, dissolving forces, replacing forces, if you will; but then it was that the broad lines of the English system set firmly. [5]

The English Revolution was not a social revolution in the sense of the French Revolution of 1789 or the Russian Revolution of 1917, but it was a political revolution in that it inaugurated the sovereignty of the people and the permanence of Parliament. From now onwards Parliament would meet regularly, as an institution not simply convened at the whim of the monarch; this was a far-reaching change.

For some years Defoe prospered, applying himself with great seriousness and energy to his business and becoming increasingly fascinated with the romance of trade. He was admitted as a liveryman of the City of London – a sure sign that he had 'arrived' as a merchant of standing – and possessed a country house as well as his London home. He diversified his operations into shipbuilding, marine insurance, land deals and civet cats (bred for a secretion used in the making of perfume). But he overreached himself. A combination of youthful impetuosity, inexperience and sheer bad luck led to a deterioration in his fortunes, and he had the chagrin of seeing the business empire he had laboriously built up encounter serious financial difficulties. There was an adventurous streak in his nature, typified by the fact that had he deserted his wife and business for a time to support the Duke of Monmouth's rebellion – an abortive attempt to organise an insurrection against King James II – and as a result was for some months a wanted man. War broke out between Britain and France, and he suffered severe losses when ships carrying his merchandise were seized by the French. He was unwise enough to invest substantial sums in risky speculative ventures and became involved in a number of expensive lawsuits when he could not honour his business promises. As a result of the war many tradesmen became bankrupt and this inevitably had repercussions on Defoe's business, for he had interests in so many different directions. The cumulative effect of these speculations and disasters was Defoe's bankruptcy in 1692 with debts of £17,000.

Later, in *The Complete English Tradesman*, he wrote of 'the miserable, anxious, perplexed life, which the poor tradesman lives under before he breaks; the distresses and extremities of his declining state; how harassed and tormented for money; what shifts he is driven to for supporting himself'.[6] These words are written with real feeling, for they are based on bitter personal experience. The impact of his bankruptcy on Defoe and his family can only be imagined. He made heroic efforts to pay off his debts, coming to an agreement with his creditors to pay all that he owed over a period of time. He acquired some marshland at Tilbury and for some years operated a profitable factory making bricks and pantiles. By 1705 he had reduced his liabilities to £5000 and recovered something of his self-esteem, though he was never again to be a London merchant on the scale of his early years as a wholesaler.

Defoe never lost his fascination with trade – he wrote later that 'Writing upon trade was the whore I really doated upon' – and his years as a businessman shaped him indelibly as a writer.[7] It was through his experiences as a tradesman that he acquired his store of knowledge on all manner of curious topics and his extensive interest in human character. As a direct result of his experience he became engrossed in domestic and overseas politics, never far below the surface of his pamphlets and essays, and travelled widely throughout Britain, gaining impressions he was to use in his novels and in the *Tour*. Most importantly, when he came to write his fictional narratives he was able to root them in a recognisable contemporary setting instead of in a fabulous past (as with Rabelais) or a mythical landscape (as with Bunyan).

Towards the end of the century he was referred to as 'Daniel de Foe' for the first time and began to adopt this style when signing his name. It is easy to infer from this that he felt the prefix 'De' made his name sound more aristocratic, but too much should not be read into this change of style. It was after all an easy transition from 'D. Foe' – his usual signature – to 'Defoe', and there is no evidence that he or his contemporaries attached much importance to the matter. Clearly he liked the sound of the prefix or he would not have adopted it, but he continued to be referred to as 'Daniel Foe' for many years after the change first appeared.

What is much more significant is that from the end of the century onwards he was increasingly preoccupied with literary work in the form of pamphlets, broadsheets and essays. *An Essay upon Projects*, his first book, was published in 1698. This was a carefully written outline for a series of ambitious projects, including a modernised road system, improved schemes for pensions and insurance, and academies for military studies and the education of women. Though out of print today, the *Essay upon Projects* is an important indication of the modernity of Defoe's thinking, his fascination with sociology and with schemes for the amelioration of the life of his time. This was followed by a prolific series of pamphlets on topical issues, including *The True-born Englishman* (1701), a poem defending William of Orange against the xenophobia of many of his contemporaries, and *Legion's Memorial* (1701) which castigated the House of Commons for its failure to vote war supplies to William.

The late seventeenth and early eighteenth centuries were a period of intense partisanship on social, political and religious issues, and consequently a time of acrimonious journalism. Newspapers and pamphlets bristled with controversy on the leading issues of the day: conformity or dissent; Whig or Tory; Stuart or Hanover; isolation or involvement in Europe; toleration of minorities or persecution. Defoe could rarely resist an opportunity to burst into print on any of these issues, but in 1702 his taste for polemical argument landed him in hot water. In December of that year he published an anonymous pamphlet, *The Shortest Way with the Dissenters*, which purported to be written by a high-church zealot advocating the most extreme punitive measures against dissenters. It was ironical in intent, for his object was to expose the intolerance and bigotry of those favouring persecution, but the pamphlet misfired. Fanatics applauded it for saying what they had long felt in private, whilst dissenters condemned it for its outspokenness. When its true authorship became known, a storm broke over Defoe's head. He was arrested in May 1703, accused of having written and published a seditious libel. He was fined, condemned to stand in the pillory, and sent to Newgate Prison 'during the Queen's pleasure'. This meant that during the busiest months of the year, when he should have been occupied with his brick business at Tilbury, he was in confinement. When he was released in November he found that his factory had come to grief and he was bankrupt for a second time. Now, at the age of 43, he would have to begin his life afresh.

At this point he was approached by Robert Harley, Speaker of the House of Commons and an influential figure in government affairs. Unlike Defoe, Harley was not a Whig but he was a man of moderation; he respected Defoe's literary abilities and felt the latter could be useful to the government. He invited Defoe to serve as a confidential agent – a 'secret agent' as he would be termed today. His function would be to travel throughout the country reporting back to Harley on the political temper of the counties; to disseminate propaganda on behalf of official policies; and to help pave the way for the union between England and Scotland, which eventually became a reality in 1707. Defoe served in this capacity from 1703 to 1714. By temperament he was well suited to this work, and he took his duties seriously. He wrote long letters to Harley recording his impressions, published numerous anonymous pamphlets supporting moderate policies, and gathered a rich mine of material that he was to use many years later in the *Tour through the Whole Island of Great Britain*.

In February 1704 he published the first number of his periodical *The Review*. Originally it was a weekly publication, but it soon changed to twice weekly and then to three times a week. It continued to be published regularly until June 1713. Theoretically Defoe was the editor of *The Review* but in practice he was the sole contributor, writing commentary and discussion on a range of topical issues: trade, religion, politics and international affairs. It was a journal of comment rather than a newspaper in the same sense as the *London Gazette*, and it is apparent that both Defoe and Harley regarded it as a mouthpiece for moderate views broadly in support of government policies. *The Review* had an estimated circulation of 400–500 copies per issue (compared with 6000 copies for the *London Gazette*), but this simply represents the number of individual copies sold. It exercised an influence out of all proportion to its circulation, for it was widely read, discussed and handed on in coffee-houses and taverns, and was even read aloud in the streets. His achievement in writing *The Review* single-handed over a ten-year period is remarkable, not only for the sheer labour involved (when it was published in facsimile in 1938 it ran to 22 volumes) but because he succeeded consistently in writing on a wide range of subjects in an entertaining, readable style. More importantly for the future author of *Robinson Crusoe*, he became adept at writing scenes and conversations in which he assumed an imaginary persona. *The Review* was the workshop in which he perfected his style as a man of reason with an ear for the speech of ordinary people.

With the death of Queen Anne and the accession of George I in 1714 the political scene was transformed. The Tory administration which Harley had served for so many years fell from office, to be replaced by a Whig government. Defoe soon adjusted himself to the new situation and continued until 1730 to serve successive Whig ministries through his journalistic activities. He became a regular contributor to *Mist's Weekly Journal*, an influential newspaper with a circulation of 10,000 copies – a large circulation for that time – writing editorials, news paragraphs and translations of items from foreign journals. *Mist's* was a virulent anti-Whig journal, and Defoe, whilst posing as a Tory, was careful to tone down its asperities and shape his contributions in such a way as to minimise its offence to the government. In addition to his prolific journalism during these years he found time to write a manual of moral and religious instruction, published in two volumes between 1715 and 1718 under the title *The Family Instructor*. The book consists of a series of dialogues between members of imaginary families and, though unpalatable to present-day taste – to a modern reader it would seem unduly and pompously moralising – it is significant as an early example of his narrative gifts. In writing *The Family Instructor* he gained valuable experience in handling conversation and, since each dialogue is linked with passages of narrative and comment, he learned to master many techniques which would be of service to him as a novelist. He learned the art of conversing with the reader in a familiar and intimate way, of creating credible characters, of writing sequences of convincing dialogue and argument, of writing stories designed with a didactic intention.

The book sold well and earned for Defoe a new reputation as a writer of popular manuals. The first decades of the eighteenth century were unusually favourable for the publication of journal-ism of this kind. Richard Steele's *Tatler* had been founded in 1709 and Joseph Addison's *Spectator* in 1711. These became immensely influential as popular miscellanies of news and comment and helped to create a market for magazines, reviews and digests. They helped to satisfy a growing thirst for knowledge: a thirst fed by a proliferation of histories, biographies and encyclopaedias. There was an increasing demand for well-written criticism, for digests of history, travel and fact presented in a lively and readable form. Defoe, with his background of journalism and experience of the real world, was well placed to meet this demand.

In 1719 he published *Robinson Crusoe*, a book which has been described as 'the first long piece of prose fiction that had the primary purpose of giving the illusion of reality'.[8] In turning from religious and political controversy to the writing of tales of adven-ture he was, in the eyes of his contemporaries, coming down in the world. It was not simply that adventure stories were regarded as demeaning in the polite world of letters, but that fiction itself was considered to be 'non-serious' by comparison with poetry, history and *belles-lettres*. It is this which helps to explain the attitude of sus-picion and resentment with which he was regarded by many of the literati of his time. For Defoe did not correspond to the respectable image of an eighteenth-century man of letters. He was not a gentle-man; his background was not in literature, but in trade. True, he had had considerable writing experience, but this was in popular journalism rather than polite letters. In this sense he was the antithesis of Pope and Swift and was regarded by them with suspi-cion and disapproval.

Robinson Crusoe was published at the price of five shillings: quite a high sum for those days. Despite its price it sold very well indeed and, in addition to its legitimate sale, soon began to appear in pirated and abridged editions. He was reaching a new public, a public eager for stories of travel and adventure written in a fluent, conversational style. Though ignored by book collectors and schol-ars, it was widely read by the newly literate artisans and workmen searching for readable, convincingly written narratives. The rise of literacy, improvements in printing techniques and the growth of popular journalism combined to create a climate extremely favourable to the kind of narratives Defoe was uniquely qualified to write. Above all, the rise of urban communities meant that there was a growing stratum of the population with the leisure and ability to read and they wished to absorb stories featuring characters with whom they could identify. All these factors helped to give birth to the modern novel.

Robinson Crusoe was rapidly followed by two sequels, then by *Memoirs of a Cavalier* (1720), *Captain Singleton* (1720), *Moll Flanders* (1722), *A Journal of the Plague Year* (1722), *Colonel Jack* (1722) and *Roxana* (1724). After 1724 he ceased to write fiction, for reasons that are still not clearly understood. Perhaps he felt he had 'written himself out'; perhaps he wearied of writing narratives of this kind and wished to return to non-fiction. The remainder of his life was spent in the composition of works of edification, a genre for which he had long had a flair. First came his massive work of topography, *A Tour through the Whole Island of Great Britain*, a summary of the impressions he had gleaned from many years of journeying through England, Scotland and Wales. This was followed by *The Complete English Tradesman*, a handbook on the complexities of running a business, which is still readable and interesting today. He then turned his attention to the supernatural, a subject which held for him a lifelong fascination. In *The Political History of the Devil*, *A System of Magic* and *An Essay on the History and Reality of Apparitions* he showed his awareness of the popular interest in ghosts and demons and sought to produce manuals of exposition which would distinguish between spurious phenomena and occurrences that were genuinely inexplicable. In 1728, when he was 68, came his last major work on trade, *A Plan of the English Commerce*. Though he was now tired and often in considerable pain from gout he was still capable of writing fluently and lucidly. To the end he continued to write manuals, pamphlets, essays and summaries revealing his gift for presenting large masses of information in an easily digestible form. The last years of his life were spent in writing and revising a lengthy work abounding in anecdotes and homilies, *The Complete English Gentleman*, a book which he clearly intended to be the definitive guide to a life of culture and respectability.

For some years he had been living quietly and comfortably at Stoke Newington, not far from his old school. His son-in-law recorded that he had built himself 'a very handsome house, as a retirement from London, and amused his time either in the cultivation of a large and pleasant garden, or in the pursuit of his studies, which he found means of making very profitable'.[9] Here he spent his time writing and reading – he had amassed a considerable library, since he had for many years developed a habit of buying rather than borrowing books – and thinking over his long and varied life. It would be pleasant to record that Defoe ended his days in these genteel surroundings. Instead, death came to him on 26 April 1731 at a lodging-house in Ropemakers Alley, London, where he had been living for some months, apparently in hiding from one of his creditors. He is buried in Bunhill Fields, Finsbury, where he lies in the same cemetery as John Bunyan and William Blake. In 1870 the plain stone that marked his grave was replaced by a marble pillar erected from the subscriptions of 1700 children in gratitude to the author of *Robinson Crusoe*.

Had Defoe died in 1718, before writing *Robinson Crusoe*, it is doubtful whether he would be remembered today, except as a footnote in history textbooks as the author of *The Shortest Way with the Dissenters* and *The Review*. As it is, his name is known throughout the world as the author of *Robinson Crusoe* and the handful of fictional narratives which he composed in his sixties. There is little evidence that Defoe was aware of the implications of what he was doing when he turned from polemical journalism to the writing of fiction. He was certainly not conscious at the time that in writing *Robinson Crusoe* and *Moll Flanders* he was creating the first novels in English and paving the way for a host of successors, including Richardson, Fielding and Smollett. The paradox is that by writing these 'non-serious' works he has earned for himself a permanent place in literary history. The great bulk of his immense output of essays, handbooks, pamphlets and outlines is completely forgotten today. But his novels are alive and well. These continue to be read and enjoyed, and will carry his name into futurity.

Defoe's Literary Achievement

The death of a major writer is usually followed by a period of reaction in which critical interest in that writer's work is at a low ebb. This phase is then succeeded by a process of rehabilitation, sometimes lasting one or even two generations. In Defoe's case, the process has been an unusually slow one, for it was not until the mid-twentieth century – more than two centuries after his death – that he became the subject of serious academic scrutiny.

During his lifetime he was regarded primarily as a pamphleteer and journalist rather than an imaginative writer. Indeed, his name did not appear on the title-page of any of his full-length works of fiction, for in his own day his reputation rested on his career as a poet and polemicist. His obituary in *The Universal Spectator* of 1 May 1731 stated simply: 'A few days ago died Daniel Defoe, Senr., a person well known for his numerous writings.' It was as a well-known author of 'numerous writings' – particularly *The Review*, *The True-Born Englishman*, *The Shortest Way with the Dissenters* and *Jure Divino* – that he was regarded by his contemporaries and the generations immediately following him. It was not until the nineteenth century that he began to receive attention as a creative writer *per se*, with Scott, Coleridge and Charles Lamb arguing powerfully in his defence. It was Sir Walter Scott who wrote a long introduction to a collected edition of his novels published in 1810, reviewing Defoe's literary career and drawing attention to his unusual qualities of characterisation. Of *Robinson Crusoe*, for example, Scott wrote that 'the author has, with wonderful exactness, described him as acting and thinking precisely as such a man must have thought and acted in such an extraordinary situation'.[10] Scott praised Defoe's narrative powers, his impressive realism and the conviction of his first-person narrators. Later in the century Stevenson, in an influential essay 'A Gossip on Romance' (reprinted in *Memories and Portraits*, 1887), praised *Robinson Crusoe* in fulsome terms, stating pertinently that 'a little story of a shipwrecked sailor, with not a tenth part of the style nor a thousandth part of the wisdom...goes on from edition to edition, ever young, while *Clarissa* lies upon the shelves unread'.

Defoe's literary standing in the first half of the twentieth century was the subject of sharp differences of opinion. Virginia Woolf in *The Common Reader* (1925) discussed Defoe as a major writer meriting serious consideration, asserting that *Moll Flanders* and *Roxana* 'stand among the few English novels which we can call indisputably great'.[11] Q. D. Leavis, on the other hand, in *Fiction and the Reading Public* (1932), dismissed him as a writer who 'concentrated on literary devices which actually preclude the creation of a work of art'. She went on:

> Contemporary critics are inclined to credit him with an artistry which he never possessed. But he was no artist, and as a journalist all his conscious ingenuity was directed to trying the pass off fiction as fact; to us his journalistic arts seem childishly cunning, transparent, and spasmodic, not psychological and insidious like those of our own age.[12]

Pat Rogers has pointed out that the significance of such comments lies not so much in the specific contentions made for or against Defoe as in the sense of engagement – 'the recognition, in a word, that Defoe repaid adult and sensitive reading'.[13] What was new in twentieth-century criticism of Defoe was the engagement with his novels *as novels* and not simply as romances or fabrications. Nevertheless, for some years the received view of his work leaned much more to Leavis than to Woolf. Henry James, for example, claimed that *Robinson Crusoe* 'isn't a novel at all' and that first-person narration 'has no authority, no persuasive or convincing force – its grasp of reality and truth isn't strong and disinterested'.[14] When F. R. Leavis came to write *The Great Tradition* in 1948 he extolled the merits of Jane Austen, George Eliot, Henry James and Joseph Conrad as exemplifying 'the great tradition' in English literature but Defoe (along with Sterne and Hardy) was excluded from the hierarchy.

The turning of the tide came with the publication of three critical works in rapid succession: A. D. McKillop's *Early Masters of English Fiction* (1956), Ian Watt's *The Rise of the Novel* (1957), and J. R. Moore's *Daniel Defoe: Citizen of the Modern Word* (1958). These works, through their sustained attention to the literary and imaginative qualities of his fiction, mark the beginning of serious modern study of Defoe as a creative writer. The explanation for the slowness of scholarly recognition of his work is not hard to find. In his own day he was a populist author, writing for a newly literate public highly readable and entertaining stories that were clearly designed to please and enlighten. His very popularity with the reading public has militated against his critical acceptance. There remains a widespread feeling that a book which provides entertainment with the minimum of effort on the part of the reader must be escapism rather than literature. That *Robinson Crusoe* is still widely regarded as a book for children rather than adults and has for many years provided the basis of a pantomime, has hindered rather than helped his critical reputation.

For decades he occupied a peripheral niche on the fringe of university studies (a dubious honour he shared with R. L. Stevenson, and for much the same reasons), largely because he was not felt to be an appropriate subject for critical scrutiny. Moreover, Defoe was paying the price for having written far too much and too unevenly. Even when allowances are made for doubtful or mistaken attributions, the bibliography of his writings amounts to well over 500 separate publications. It is not merely his prolifigacy which is daunting but his range, embracing as it does fiction, prophecy, biography, topography, theology, poetry and polemic. Because of this diversity it has been difficult to know under which rubric to classify him. He *was* a novelist certainly, but he was many other things besides, including a tradesman, a journalist and a secret agent.

In all this he has much in common with H. G. Wells. Like Wells, he is difficult to classify, suspect because of his popularity, and hampered by his extreme discursiveness. Like Wells, his reputation has suffered because of the uneven quality of his work. He was capable of producing such works as *Robinson Crusoe*, *Moll Flanders* and *Roxana*: brilliant myths that have profoundly influenced English literature. In *A Journal of the Plague Year* and the *Tour through the Whole Island of Great Britain* he forged a distinctive documentary style which deeply affected later writers, including Wells and Orwell. But he was also capable of such lack-lustre productions as *The Further Adventures of Robinson Crusoe* and *The Political History of the Devil*, works that have done little to enhance his reputation and, in the eyes of many, merely confirmed the image of a hack writer who could turn his hand to any form of literary expression. Had he been content to write a smaller number of works of more consistent quality, the recognition of his stature might not have been such a slow process.

We now turn to Defoe's significance in the development of the novel. We shall discuss, first, his role in initiating the tradition of realism in the English novel; secondly, look at his influence on later writers, especially Stevenson, Wells and Orwell; and thirdly, review the significance of the 'desert island' myth. The remainder of the chapter will raise three questions: Is any pattern discernible in his work? Is there any development in his fiction? What are his limitations as a novelist? We shall conclude with a summary of his importance to the modern world.

Defoe is widely regarded as the inventor of the English novel and the pioneer of the realist tradition within it. Prior to the publication of *Robinson Crusoe* in 1719 the realist novel in England was virtually unknown. Bunyan's *The Pilgrim's Progress* was published in 1678 and Mrs Aphra Behn's *Oroonoko* in 1688, but neither of these can be regarded as a realist novel in the same sense as Defoe's narratives. What was new about his work was its extraordinary verisimilitude, his ability to create convincing fictional worlds. It is not surprising that there has long been a debate as to whether *Robinson Crusoe* and *Moll Flanders* are 'true' novels (that is, in the Jamesian sense of having a 'commanding centre') or whether they are romances. The uncertainty stems from the fact that his narratives possess some of the characteristics of both. Much of Defoe's skill as a creative writer lies in his fusion of the ordinary and the romantic, his gift of combining matter-of-fact detail with description of unusual or striking events. Whether he is describing Crusoe's obsessive determination to bake bread or fire pottery, Moll's resolve to pursue a career of petty crime or Jack's quest in search of his true self, we are impressed by his deft combination of the prosaic and the unusual.

The following passage from *Robinson Crusoe*, selected at random, will serve as an illustration of his technique:

> All the Remedy that offer'd to my Thoughts at that Time, was, to get up into a thick bushy Tree like a Fir, but thorny, which grew near me, and where I resolv'd to set all Night, and consider the next Day what Death I should dye, for as yet I saw no Prospect of Life; I walk'd about a Furlong from the Shore, to see if I could find any fresh Water to drink, which I did, to my great Joy; and having drank and put a little Tobacco in my Mouth to prevent

Hunger, I went to the Tree, and getting up into it, endeavour'd to place my self so, as that if I should sleep I might not fall; and having cut me a short Stick, like a Truncheon, for my Defence, I took up my Lodging, and having been excessively fatigu'd, I fell fast asleep, and slept as comfortably as, I believe, few could have done in my Condition, and found my self the most refresh'd with it, that I think I ever was on such an Occasion.   (p. 47)

The passage contains many touches characteristic of Defoe. We note the conversational, rather rambling style – the paragraph consists of 180 words strung together in a single sentence. We note, too, the fondness for biblical language – 'to my great Joy', 'found my self the most refresh'd '. The passage contains a number of homely phrases which assist the reader to identify with the narrator – 'I resolv'd to set all Night', 'I took up my Lodging', 'I fell fast asleep'. Notice also the skilful use of tense: 'having drank and put a little Tobacco in my Mouth', 'having cut me a short Stick'. Crusoe is describing events which have occurred in the past, but they are recounted so vividly that it is as if he is describing incidents happening here and now. The narrative is interspersed with points of detail possessing all the reality of an actual location: 'a thick bushy Tree like a Fir'; 'which grew near me'; 'I walk'd about a Furlong from the Shore'. These fix the scene in the mind with the clarity of a still photograph.

The effect is threefold: (a) the reader is convinced of the truth of Crusoe's narrative; (b) he shares vicariously in Crusoe's adventures and reflections; and (c) he can visualise the scene clearly in the imagination. The style is matter-of-fact, almost pedestrian, yet it is surprisingly effective. It achieves its impact without elegance or any consciously 'literary' touches; the very simplicity of Defoe's language seems to guarantee its truth. The apparent simplicity is deceptive: the style was arrived at after years of experience as a journalist and editor and is admirably suited to his purpose – to convey the thoughts, moods and actions of an ordinary person in adverse circumstances.

When we say a novel is 'realistic' we do not simply mean that it is rich in circumstantial detail but that it contains conversations and incidents that are true to everyday life. This was well within Defoe's capabilities. The dialogue in his early fiction tends to be somewhat stilted, but as he gained confidence he became increasingly skilled at the presentation of conversations possessing the ring of truth.

Consider, for example, the following exchange between husband and wife (the wife has noticed that her husband is melancholy and she is determined to find the explanation for his behaviour):

'My dear, what is the matter with you?'
'Nothing.'
'Nay, don't put me off with an answer that signifies nothing; tell me what is the matter, for I am sure something extraordinary is the case – tell me, I say, do tell me.' (Then she kisses him.)
'Prithee, don't trouble me.'
'I will know what is the matter.'
'I tell you nothing is the matter – what should be the matter?'
'Come, my dear, I must not be put off so; I am sure, if it be any thing ill, I must have my share of it; and why should I not be worthy to know it, whatever it is, before it comes upon me.'
'Poor woman!' (He kisses her.)
'Well, but let me know what it is; come, don't distract yourself alone; let me bear a share of your grief, as well as I have shared in your joy.'
'My dear, let me alone, you trouble me now, indeed.' (Still he keeps her off.)
'Then you will not trust your wife with knowing what touches you so sensibly?'
'I tell you, it is nothing, it is a trifle, it is not worth talking of.'
'Don't put me off with such stuff as that; I tell you, it is not for nothing that you have been so concerned, and that so long too; I have seen it plain enough; why, you have drooped upon it for this fortnight past, and above.'
'Ay, this twelvemonth, and more.'
'Very well, and yet it is nothing.'
'It is nothing that you can help me in.'
'Well, but how do you know that? Let me see, and judge whether I can, or no.'
'I tell you, you cannot.'
'Sure it is some terrible thing then. Why must not I know it? What! are you going to break? Come, tell me the worst of it.'
'Break! no, no, I hope not – Break! no, I'll never break.'
'As good as you have broke; don't presume; no man in trade can say he won't break.'

(*The Complete English Tradesman*, chapter xi)

Such an exchange could only have been written as a result of close observation of human fraillties. Throughout their dialogue one is conscious of the wife's determination to arrive at the truth and of his equally firm resolve to keep the explanation to himself. She uses all her guile to persuade him to be frank, beginning with a simple question ('what is the matter with you?'), moving on to a demand ('I will know what is the matter'), next reason ('I must not be put off so'), then compassion ('let me bear a share of your grief'). When she complains that he has been out of sorts for a fortnight past he replies: 'Ay, this twelvemonth and more', to which she replies tellingly: 'Very well, and yet it is nothing.' The quiet force of this riposte is the stuff of which real-life conversations are made. At each evasion of her probing, the husband becomes visibly more uncomfortable: 'don't trouble me', 'nothing is the matter', 'let me alone', 'you trouble me now', 'it is not worth talking of'. The passage as a whole is a striking instance of Defoe's ability to record not simply the words of a dialogue but its spirit and nuances. When he adds in parenthesis: 'Still he keeps her off', we are aware of the barrier dividing husband and wife. She *knows* within herself that she is right to demand an explanation; he is uneasily aware that by failing to be candid he has wronged her.

In his interesting study *Defoe's Fiction*, Ian Bell has commented:

> All tales are constructions, selecting items for emphasis, and distorting chronology for some purpose. But the mimetic work does not draw readers into seeing this. It pretends instead that the conventions are transparent, and that they are not conventions at all, but windows to the world.[15]

In this sense Defoe's narratives are the antithesis of self-reflective novels such as Sterne's *Tristram Shandy* (1759–67) or John Fowles's *The French Lieutenant's Woman* (1969). They are, by contrast, 'windows to the world' and do not draw attention to their own fictiveness. When reading a Defoe novel we continually have to remind ourselves that we are reading an artificial construct, so vivid is the world depicted. The figure who comes most readily to mind in this connection is Dickens, who greatly admired Defoe and shared his ability to create totally realistic fictional worlds. (*Robinson Crusoe* is one of the 'glorious host' of books which console David Copperfield in his unhappiness when he is punished by his stepfather: see *David Copperfield*, chapter iv.) It was precisely this point that Virginia Woolf had in mind when she wrote: 'It never occurred to us that there was such a person as Defoe, and to have been told that *Robinson Crusoe* was the work of a man with a pen in his hand would either have disturbed us unpleasantly or meant nothing at all.'[16] In other words, the effect of realism is an allusion, and once the illusion is pointed out to us it comes as a disillusionment. To learn that *Crusoe* is a wholly imaginary account would destroy the myth Defoe has been at such pains to sustain.

It may be objected that Defoe's narratives are not novels in the Jamesian or Leavisian sense but works of reportage; that what is presented is merely a journalistic impression masquerading as fiction. But close examination of his narratives (as will be demonstrated in the chapters which follow) does not support this view. For in considering Defoe we are faced with the question: how do we account for his continuing popularity? Today all his major works of fiction are available in well-edited critical editions; they continue to be read, studied and enjoyed not only in schools and universities but by ordinary readers. It is difficult to explain this popularity if Defoe was merely an author of works of reportage. The explanation surely lies in the fact that he was the supreme realist; that the reader identifies with his heroes and heroines, relates to them and sympathises with them in their journey through life. The reader is a participant in an adventure, identifying with the narrator through all his experiences. In achieving this effect Defoe transformed the English novel from the picaresque romance to the novel of character, focusing with growing intensity on the personality, attitudes and thoughts of the autobiographical narrator. In doing so he imposed coherence on the novel, establishing for the genre a realistic frame of reference firmly rooted in time and place. It is in the creation of this sense of realism – the conviction that what is being described actually happened to a living person in a familiar location – that he made his most distinctive contribution to the development of the novel.

It has been remarked of Defoe that he was one of the initiators of the 'romantic adventure tradition' and that 'his successors are not Richardson and Fielding, but Stevenson and Scott, and a host of forgotten popular authors'.[17] By this is meant that he was one of the earliest practitioners of the novel of escapism, the adventure-narrative in which the hero or heroine embarks on a quest, contending with the unknown. Without necessarily subscribing to this view in its entirety we may certainly agree that Stevenson was one of Defoe's successors and that *Treasure Island* and *The Ebb-Tide*, for example, have a deep emotional affinity with *Robinson Crusoe*. What Stevenson and Defoe have in common is the pictorial quality of their imagination: their ability to describe a scene with such intensity that it is fixed indelibly in the mind. If one thinks of Crusoe's landing on his island or his first sight of Friday's footprint, one visualises the scene with all the clarity of a photograph – every detail impinges on the imagination. The same is true of the landing of the *Hispaniola* in *Treasure Island*, the flight through the heather in *Kidnapped* or the dual between the Durie brothers in *The Master of Ballantrae*. Each of these scenes is depicted with total conviction, as if the events described have actually occurred. It is this pictorial quality that Stevenson had in mind when he wrote:

> The author must know his countryside, whether real or imaginary, like his hand; the distances, the points of the compass, the place of the sun's rising, the behaviour of the moon, should all be beyond cavil.[18]

Because Stevenson could *see* the landscape before him when writing *Treasure Island* the reader has a crystal-clear picture of the terrain: it is described with the realism and attention to detail of an actual location. Because Defoe could see Crusoe's island in his mind's eye he knew every detail of its landscape – its hills, valleys, trees and coves. Both writers could communicate this sense of reality in limpid prose which enabled their readers to share their sense of immediacy and participation. In Stevenson's comparison of *Robinson Crusoe* and *Clarissa* quoted above he concludes by noting that '*Clarissa* has every quality that can be shown in prose, one alone excepted – pictorial or picture-making romance.' In the same essay he observes that the reading process should be 'absorbing and voluptuous: we should gloat over a book, be rapt clean out of ourselves, and rise from the perusal, our mind filled with the busiest, kaleidoscopic dance of images'. This emphasis on visual elements, on a 'dance of images' which would totally absorb the reader, was Defoe's clearest legacy and one which has inspired generations of writers including Dickens, Poe (most notably in *The*

Narrative of Arthur Gordon Pym) and John Buchan. Stevenson also
noted that the difference between Defoe's novel and Richardson's
lay in the fact that *Crusoe* depends for the most part 'on the charm
of circumstance'. Stevenson learned much from Defoe, not least the
ability to charm the reader by the accumulation of homely circum-
stantiality.

Reference has already been made to the similarities between
Defoe and Wells. Both were didactic novelists with a strong sense of
the role of the novel as a vehicle for the discussion of ideas; both
were much more at home in the discursive tradition than in the
conception of the novel as a harmoniously constructed work of art;
and both regarded the genre as an infinitely flexible form which
could accommodate fictionalised autobiography, documentary,
travel adventure and confessional. When Wells proclaimed that the
novel is a 'powerful instrument of moral suggestion' and that it
should 'discuss conduct, analyse conduct, suggest conduct, illuminate it through and through',[19] Defoe would undoubtedly have
concurred. *Robinson Crusoe*, *Moll Flanders* and *Roxana* are novels
which discuss and illuminate conduct in the same sense that *Tono-
Bungay* and *Kipps* throw a searching light on aspects of human
behaviour. In writing their *Bildungsromans*, Defoe and Wells were
seeking to convey a presentation of human experience in all its
chaotic variety. The narrator of *Tono-Bungay* declares: 'My ideas of a
novel all through are comprehensive rather than austere.... And it
isn't a constructed tale I have to tell but unmanageable realities.'[20]
How well Defoe would have understood the urge towards discursiveness, the sense of life as a chaos that cannot be contained within
a neat, symmetrical narrative.

There are many superficial similarities between the two writers:
their liking for novels told in the first person; their fondness for lists
(witness the list of items Crusoe succeeds in retrieving from the
wreck, and the itemisation of the contents of the ship's pantry in
Wells's *Mr Blettsworthy on Rampole Island*); their ability to turn their
hands to a diverse range of literary forms. Beyond these resem-
blances is another factor less easy to define. What Wells and Defoe
had in common above all else was an unusual ability to combine
the most intense personal narrative with a sombre detachment: to
be simultaneously a participant and an onlooker. One can see this
dual perspective most strikingly in *A Journal of the Plague Year* and
The War of the Worlds. The following extracts illustrate the point:

London might well be said to be all in Tears; the Mourners did not go about the Streets indeed, for no Body put on black, or made a formal Dress of Mourning for their nearest Friends; but the Voice of Mourning was truly heard in the Streets; the shriecks of Women and Children at the Windows, and Doors of their Houses, where their dearest Relations were, perhaps dying, or just dead, were so frequent to be heard, as we passed the Streets, that it was enough to pierce the stoutest Heart in the World, to hear them. Tears and Lamentations were seen almost in every House, especially in the first Part of the Visitation; for towards the latter End, Mens Hearts were hardned, and Death was so always before their Eyes, that they did not so much concern themselves for Loss of their Friends, expecting, that themselves should be summoned the next Hour.

Business led me out sometimes to the other End of the Town, even when the Sickness was chiefly there; and as the thing was new to me, as well as to every Body else, it was a most surprising thing, to see those Streets, which were usually so thronged, now grown desolate, and so few People to be seen in them, that if I had been a Stranger, and at a Loss for my Way, I might sometimes have gone the Length of a whole Street, I mean of the by-Streets, and see no Body to direct me, except Watchmen, set at the Doors of such Houses as were shut up; of which I shall speak presently. (*Journal of the Plague Year*, pp. 16–17)

For some time I stood tottering on the mound, regardless of my safety. Within that noisome den from which I had emerged, I had thought with a narrow intensity only of our immediate security. I had not realized what had been happening to the world, had not anticipated this startling vision of unfamiliar things. I had expected to see Sheen in ruins – I found about me the landscape, weird and lurid, of another planet.

For that moment I touched an emotion beyond the common range of men, yet one that the poor brutes we dominate know only too well. I felt as a rabbit might feel returning to his burrow, and suddenly confronted by the work of a dozen busy navvies digging the foundations of a house. I felt the first inkling of a thing that presently grew quite clear in my mind, that oppressed me for many days, a sense of dethronement, a persuasion that I was no longer a master, but an animal among the animals, under the Martian heel. With us it would be as with them, to lurk and watch, to run and hide; the fear and empire of man had passed away. (*War of the Worlds*, Book 2, 6)

In both passages the reader is aware of an individual voice commenting and participating in the story: 'Business led me out sometimes', 'the thing was new to me', 'of which I shall speak presently', 'For some time I stood tottering on the mound', 'I had expected to see Sheen in ruins'. At the same time we are conscious of a detachment which enables the narrator to view the action of the story from the outside: 'London might well be said to be all in Tears', 'the Voice of Mourning was truly heard in the Streets', 'the fear and empire of man had passed away'. What the two passages have in common is a feeling of *alienation*, of being a witness to events beyond the normal experience of man. When the narrator of the *Journal* remarks that 'Mens Hearts were hardned, and Death was so always before their Eyes' and goes on to describe the desolation of the streets, he is struggling to convey sights and sounds beyond everyday experience. Wells terms this feeling 'a sense of dethronement, a persuasion that I was ... an animal among the animals'. It is this ability to view London and mankind from the perspective of an onlooker that he and Defoe had in common – to awaken the reader to a sense of disaster overwhelming the human species.

In his essay *The English People* George Orwell remarked apropos of the English language:

Language ought to be the joint creation of poets and manual workers, and in modern England it is difficult for these two classes to meet. When they can do so again – as, in a different way, they could in the feudal past – English may show more clearly than at present its kinship with the language of Shakespeare and Defoe.[21]

It is significant that what attracts Orwell about Defoe is his *language*. Both Defoe and Orwell had a liking for plain statement and a dislike of circumlocution. Both possessed an honest, plodding, dispassionate voice characterised by simplicity and directness. Beyond this, both were consumed with curiosity concerning the lives and habits of ordinary people and both wrote works of reportage which combine an overview of society at a fixed point in time with intense curiosity about individual lives. The Defoe of *A Journal of the Plague*

Year and the *Tour* has much in common with the Orwell of *Down and Out in Paris and London* and *The Road to Wigan Pier*. All four works are notable for their directness of language and insight into the motivations and behaviour of inconspicuous people. Through all his years of experience as a journalist Defoe consciously strove to achieve a plain and homely style. In the preface to *Serious Reflections of Robinson Crusoe* he declared:

> The plainness I profess, both in style and method, seems to have some suitable analogy to the subject, honesty, and therefore is absolutely necessary to be strictly followed; and I must own, I am the better reconciled, on this very account, to a natural infirmity of homely plain writing . . . .

This plainness of style was perfected throughout his long career as a journalist and editor of *The Review* and is best seen in the homely scenes and incidents which fill the pages of *Robinson Crusoe*. It is a style which relies for its effect on an extensive use of biblical cadences, the minimum use of foreign words and phrases, and a conversational manner which creates the illusion that what is being described is happening while the words are being written. It is a style which relies heavily on the tactile: on the shape, feel and texture of everyday things – furniture, houses, rooms, purses, coins, tools.

Orwell was also a conscious stylist, fashioning a distinctive tone of writing through a long apprenticeship as essayist and reviewer. His standing today and during his lifetime rests largely on the honesty of his style: on his determination to tell the truth as he saw it; to convey the atmosphere of rooms, dwellings, public houses, lodgings. Whether describing a descent down a coal-mine, a sojourn in a lodging-house, his experiences as a dishwasher in a Paris hotel or hop-picking in Kent, his prose is notable for its unadorned clarity. It is a prose that is passionate, straight and candid, diametrically opposed to the 'Newspeak' of *Nineteen Eighty-Four* (a language designed to conceal rather than to communicate).

Defoe and Orwell excelled at a documentary style ideally suited to the depiction of England at a crisis in its history. Defoe in the *Journal* and Orwell in *Wigan Pier* sought to convey a panoramic view of English life by presenting an impression of the nation as a whole interwoven with vivid pictures drawn from humdrum lives.

If either of these accounts had been simply a factual summary, one doubts whether they would be read today. What brings each vividly to the imagination is the fusion of the general and the particular, the evident fascination with the occupations and attitudes of ordinary folk. In his essay 'Charles Dickens' Orwell wrote: 'When one reads any strongly individual piece of writing one has the impression of seeing a face somewhere behind the page.'[22] He feels this very strongly, he says, with Swift, Defoe, Fielding and Dickens. It is significant that he singles out Defoe for special mention as a writer possessing an individual voice whose personality animates his fiction.

The desert island myth is one of the most potent myths to haunt world literature. The numerous imitations of *Robinson Crusoe*, known generically as 'Robinsonnades', number several hundred, including Swift's *Gulivers Travels*, Wyss's *The Swiss Family Robinson* and Ballantyne's *The Coral Island*. The image of a lone survivor marooned on a virgin island has exercised a profound influence on the development of the novel and the short story and is a continuing source of reference in science fiction and fantasy.

The phrase 'desert island myth' embraces not merely the physical situation of a survivor (or survivors) on an island but the child-like aspects of Crusoe's situation, the experience of journeying through a process of trial and error from innocence to enlightenment. In order to survive in his isolation Crusoe has no alternative but to learn or re-learn a range of skills acquired by man over many generations – harvesting crops, baking bread, firing pottery, making tools. In doing so he learns by his mistakes in an essentially childlike way, advancing from naïveté to knowledge in a laborious quest for self-sufficiency. In order to cross the African continent Singleton has no alternative but to face unknown dangers by attempting a journey never previously undertaken. Neither he nor his followers have any certain knowledge of what lies ahead of them; he is a tyro embarking on a journey of exploration. In this sense Crusoe and Singleton are both innocents in a Garden of Eden, re-enacting through their experiences the transition from adolescence to adulthood. A novel such as John Fowles's *The Magus*, which on first reading would seem to have little if anything in common with *Robinson Crusoe*, can be seen on closer examination to be a modern example of the myth.[23] In both *Crusoe* and *The Magus* a lone Englishman undergoes a series of heuristic experiences on an island; in both, the protagonist is a neo-phyte in an environment to which he has continually to adapt himself; in both, the protagonist gains in maturity as a result of his experiences. Prendick in Wells's *The Island of Doctor Moreau* is also marooned on a lonely Pacific island and as a result of his sojourn has to rethink his attitudes to man and nature. The boy survivors in William Golding's *Lord of the Flies* have to learn to adapt to a world without adults and in the process learn many truths concerning themselves and each other.

Crusoe's island can be read as a metaphor for the myth of the enchanted garden, an image which can be traced through many lit-eratures and many centuries. Until his arrival the island is a natural paradise, a raw wilderness untainted by civilisation. It is Crusoe who, simply in order to survive, disturbs the pastoral tranquillity with a gun, sets traps to kill animals and disturbs the balance of nature. During his sojourn he is the horrified witness to scenes of murder and cannibalism as the island is visited by natives from the mainland. Once his solitary reign is over and he entrusts his domain to others, the island becomes a setting for treachery, greed and violence. The idea of an earthly paradise corrupted by the sudden impact of civilisation continues to exercise the imagination and can be traced through the writings of Hawthorne, Poe, Wells and many others.

The fascination of the desert island myth lies in its immense fer-tility, in the sense imparted to the reader that the situation is one of almost limitless possibilities. In reading *Crusoe* one becomes a child again because one is re-enacting the learning process. In a percep-tive comment on this point Stevenson observed: 'Fiction is to the grown man what play is to the child; it is there that he changes the atmosphere and tenor of his life.'[24] Almost all Defoe's first person narrators – Crusoe, Singleton, Moll, Jack – have this in common: that in reading their adventures one identifies with them so power-fully that one is transported to a state of receptivity. We learn with them, sharing in their misfortunes and gaining in maturity pace by pace with them. The sense of a new beginning which is an intrinsic element in the island myth is closely associated with the idea of separation from the world. Much of the charm of the first half of *Robinson Crusoe* lies in the narrator's isolation from mankind: the notion that he is in a world of his own, free to make of it what he wishes. The idea of severing oneself from all extraneous influences has exercised a powerful appeal for many writers, including Thoreau – especially in *Walden* (1854), an eloquent plea for self-sufficiency and simplicity – and can be seen in the many romances in which a lone protagonist recounts his experiences apart from his fellow men.

Defoe must have been aware of desert island myths preceding his own, most notably Shakespeare's *The Tempest* (1611). His distinctive contribution was to personalise the myth in the form of a plain, homely narrative told by a storyteller with whom readers could identify. So vividly is this done that the trappings of Crusoe's island – the goatskins, the parrot, the umbrella, the footprint – are indelibly fixed in the human consciousness. The myth of a solitary survivor painstakingly recreating a semblance of civilisation continues to haunt the imagination. That it does so in such a powerful and pictorial manner is due in large measure to the realism and conviction of his desert island tale.

If we ask the question whether any pattern or theme is discernible in Defoe's work, we come back inevitably to the question of survival. The dominant theme underlying his fiction has been defined as 'the lonely and futile search for a significant selfhood in an inhospitable and unsustaining world'.[25] The common bond uniting all his narrators is their *ordinariness*: they are essentially normal people undergoing abnormal experiences. Because each is a credible, fallible human being the reader identifies with them, willing them to survive in a hostile or indifferent universe. Crusoe has to conquer his environment simply in order to live; unless he can master the arts of husbandry he will starve. Moll has to use all her guile as a courtesan to ensure her survival in a predatory world. Jack is such an engaging picaresque hero that the reader is with him every step of the way, sharing vicariously in his adventures. Each is struggling to cope with the challenge of the present moment, adapting to circumstances in a pragmatic search for independence.

It is worth reminding ourselves that this is an essentially secular view of the human predicament. Though Defoe was brought up within the Puritan tradition and his narrators are prone to pietistic moralising, the view of life that can be deduced from his novels is one of reliance on human resourcefulness. His heroes and heroines survive against all odds because they use all their qualities of ingenuity, patience and cunning in their determination to win for themselves a place in the sun. The self-reliance which is the hallmark of their behaviour is characteristic of the rise of capitalism: indeed, it is arguable that the rise of the novel and the emergence of the mercantile age are inseparably linked. The qualities which typify Defoe's narrators – self-reliance, acumen, adaptability – are the very qualities in such demand during the birth of the modern age and which he embodied so forcefully in his own person. The spirit infusing his novels is experimentation: a willingness to adapt oneself to the vagaries of fortune and a refusal to be browbeaten by unpromising or limiting circumstances. To use a modern expression, his narrators are characterised by their upward mobility: the urge to be a gentleman, to be socially acquisitive, to better one's lot. Their primary attitude to life can be defined as a determination to make the utmost of their opportunities: a refusal to accept their lot until every possibility of advancement has been exhausted. When we examine *Robinson Crusoe* in detail we shall see that this remains true despite Crusoe's frequent appeals to the intervention of providence. Defoe's outlook on the world is fundamentally a humanist one and in pretending otherwise 'he was making prodigious efforts to deceive himself'.[26]

If Defoe's fiction is read in the order in which it was written one is irresistibly aware of a development: a progression from adventure story to novel. Through the sequence of his novels from *Robinson Crusoe* (1719) to *Roxana* (1724) a tangible enlargement in the role and significance of the narrator and an increasing sophistication in the depiction of the central character are evident. In the early novels – *Robinson Crusoe* and its sequel the *Further Adventures*, *Memoirs of a Cavalier* and *Captain Singleton* – the narrator is handled in a relatively unsophisticated way with little psychological depth. From *Moll Flanders* onwards one is conscious of a far greater psychological insight. This is partly a matter of experience: in writing one story after another in rapid succession he undoubtedly gained self-confidence in the handling of character and became more adept at conveying nuances of behaviour. But it is also a matter of choice. As his career progressed he became more and more fascinated by the possibilities inherent in the novel form and in particular by the fluidity of the first-person narrator. He came to see that the novel could depict not only outward actions but innermost thoughts. He well knew that human behaviour is often a mass of contradictions, that people often behave in an irrational manner, and that warring motives can complete for attention within the same individual. Witness Moll and Roxana who are frequently torn between unselfish and ignoble motives, or Colonel Jack who is a far more ambivalent character than Singleton or the Cavalier. In *Moll Flanders, A Journal of the Plague Year, Colonel Jack* and *Roxana* Defoe's fascination with human behaviour comes to the fore, his preoccupation with dissecting human conduct. Much of *Moll Flanders*, for example, is a dialogue between Moll and herself (or between her better and worse selves) in which she debates the wisdom of her actions and seeks to justify her behaviour to the reader.

The process attains its most mature expression in *Roxana*, which becomes not merely the story of the heroine's life but an exploration of Roxana herself, her personality and attitudes. In this sense *Roxana* is a psychological novel, exploring with subtlety and conviction the tensions and drives dividing the human temperament. Defoe had begun his novelistic career with an *idée fixe* of a hostile outer world: Crusoe and Singleton battle against an inhospitable or indifferent environment and at last gain mastery over a series of natural obstacles. Moll and Roxana also struggle against an outer world but each is also uncomfortably aware of an inner world: the narrator's own darker self. This brooding sense of a well of irrationality almost overwhelms Roxana, so much so that Defoe was unable to complete it in accordance with his original design and brought the story to an abrupt conclusion. Despite the reader's awareness that the story is truncated, it remains very much a modern novel in its tone and psychology, for Roxana is the first in a long line of characters – in the narratives of Poe, Dostoevsky, Stevenson and Kafka, for example – who are divided against themselves and tormented by self-doubt. Roxana is a believable character precisely because she is subject to the normal human frailties and emotions: remorse, chagrin, hesitation, avarice.

One can only regret that Defoe ceased to write fiction after 1724, for the logical development of his work would have been a fully rounded study of a sample human life. As it is, we have in *Moll Flanders* and *Roxana* a tantalising glimpse of what might have been. That these are still read today, 270 years after their composition, is impressive testimony to his powers as a novelist.

What are his limitations as a creative writer? For many years it was a commonplace of Defoe criticism to assert that his works lack artistic control: that he fails to exclude the irrelevant and insignificant. Thus, Lionel Stevenson in *The English Novel* deprecates him for 'the absence of customary artistic responsibility' and argues that 'in fiction we expect the irrelevant to be excluded, the significant to be intensified, and an underlying pattern of causation to be revealed'.[27] To some extent this is based on a misunderstanding of Defoe's position. Because he wished to present the diversity of human life, he felt that he had to include everything that ministered to his overall design, however seemingly unimportant. It is largely because Moll's life is so untidy – a patchwork quilt of broken marriages, fresh starts and picaresque adventures – that her story has such irresistible appeal. Defoe would have argued that human life *is* untidy, that it frequently contains inharmonious or unassimilated elements and rarely conforms to a wholly structured pattern. But it is by no means the case that his fiction is lacking in 'an underlying pattern of causation'. With few exceptions his major novels dramatise themes and ideas germane to human experience: the journey from isolation to dependence or from innocence to enlightenment; the tension between nature and civilisation, or between outward prosperity and inner doubt. His dogged accumulation of detail on every aspect of life tends to obscure the motifs underlying his first-person narratives.

His critics are on firmer ground in drawing attention to the weaknesses of his characterisation. G. H. Maynadier expressed the nub of the matter concisely:

> He had a marvellous knowledge of strange and distant lands; even in equatorial Africa he could crowd incident on incident, and make the reader believe in its reality; but he could not make his characters into human beings who moved and breathed and spoke and thought.[28]

This was written a generation before Ian Watt's *The Rise of the Novel*, and one suspects that few modern scholars would concur with this judgement without reservation. During the past 30 years there has been increasing attention to Defoe as a novelist, and a number of important critical studies have focused on aspects of his art as an imaginative writer.

But whilst we may reject Maynadier's comment as too sweeping it must be acknowledged that it contains a germ of truth. If we take any of his novels we find an almost invariable pattern: there is one character, the narrator, who is presented as a fully rounded and believable human being. That character certainly moves, breathes,

speaks and thinks. We are given a description of his or her childhood, friendships, emotional development and journey to maturity.
We learn of the vicissitudes of fortune, the social and economic
factors affecting the person's life, and their outlook on the world.
But the remaining characters in the story are usually far less solidly
drawn. By comparison with the central figure, the secondary actors
– for example, the various husbands in *Moll Flanders*, Mouchat in
Colonel Jack, Fielding in *Memoirs of a Cavalier* or the Dutch merchant
in *Roxana* – are shadowy figures, lacking in depth. They are what
E. M. Forster would have termed 'flat' characters: types or carica-
tures rather than living human beings. Moreover, Defoe's heroes
and heroines, partly because of the first-person method of narration
he invariably adopts, tend to view the exterior world and the other
characters solely from their own point of view. The result is a solip-
sistic outlook on the world, a view of life in which the sole criterion
is the well-being of the narrator. It is revealing that when Crusoe
sees the footprint in the sand his first reaction is one of abject terror
rather than of joy at the thought of human companionship. The
missing element in both *Moll Flanders* and *Roxana* is an impression
of the central character from the point of view of someone other
than herself. As it is, we only have her own word to explain her
actions and thoughts: it is difficult to arrive at a dispassionate
appraisal of her as a person since she is only seen from a single
vantage point. Had Defoe written either novel in the third person a
more balanced view of the heroine would have been possible.

As against this, it should be pointed out that Defoe goes to considerable lengths to place his protagonists in a three-dimensional
world: to ensure that they are seen in interaction with others. This
is achieved partly through reflective passages in which he or she
speculates on the motives and actions of others, and partly through
dialogue. The relationships between Singleton and William, Crusoe
and friday, and Roxana and Amy, are carefully built up through a
process of reflection and conversation in which each impinges on
the other. Defoe was feeling his way in a new and relatively untried
form, and whilst his fictions seem unsophisticated by comparison
with, say, Jane Austen or Dickens it should be remembered that he
was writing within a very different intellectual framework and at a
time when 'the novel' and its associated terminology and apparatus
of criticism were completely unknown.

His outlook on life was largely utilitarian and philistine, and this
is reflected in his work. There is little in his fiction to indicate that

he possessed any aesthetic sense regarding architecture, music or art; and whilst his conception of language is evident from his writing, it is interesting that literary criticism as such remained outside his field. He regarded himself as a journalist rather than a novelist (a term unknown at that time) and would no doubt have been deeply surprised to learn that his posthumous reputation rested on the handful of fictional narratives he composed at the end of a career crowded with activity. That these survive while the bulk of his immense output is now forgotten is because his novels, imperfect though they are, are animated with the realism and vitality of life.

Defoe's fiction is firmly rooted in human experience. His readers could relate to it because he deals with the human condition in all its confusion: with the struggle for security and self-sufficiency in a predatory and irrational world. In his seven major novels he experimented with a surprising range of genres and themes: isolation and survival (*Robinson Crusoe*); the military chronicle (*Memoirs of a Cavalier*); the journey into the unknown (*Captain Singleton*); the novel of the city (*Moll Flanders*); the disaster novel (*A Journal of the Plague Year*); the *Bildungsroman* (*Colonel Jack*); the psychological novel (*Roxana*). His overriding theme is the emergence of the modern world: the rise of the tradesman, the financier, the community, the city.

Today we live in a world in which the novel is an established literary form and has been tried and tested over a period of two and a half centuries. In considering his achievement we have to remind ourselves forcibly of the newness of the novel form at the time when he was writing. All the terminology which we take so much for granted – genre, structure, point of view, technique, symbol – was not then the commonplace of discussion. Defoe was starting more than he knew when he launched Crusoe on his journey. For he was giving birth to a fragile infant which signalled the arrival of modern civilisation. His significance for the modern world lies in this: that beginning with the publication of *Robinson Crusoe* and *Moll Flanders* there is a growing concern in fiction with the inner self, the private life of thought and reflection; and hand in hand with this is an increasing emphasis on man as a social being, a citizen in community.

The beginnings of the English novel are normally traced to Defoe because in his work we recognise distinct individuals possessing personal qualities. Crusoe and Moll both feel themselves to be individuals responsible for their own destinies – as distinct from vassals with no control over their lives – and both possess qualities of self-reliance characteristic of their time. Each has communal interests but this is combined with a strong sense of individuality. It is this sense of a private life, an inner world of thought and reverie, which distinguishes Defoe's narratives from those preceding them. For the first time we have an awareness of a central character who is not simply a type or a symbol but an *individual* prone to moods of remorse, doubt, sorrow or envy.

This introspection is balanced by a preoccupation with man as an urban being. *Moll Flanders* and *A Journal of the Plague Year* are both urban novels in the sense that London is their backcloth: both works would be immeasurably poorer without an awareness of London as a city bustling with life and commerce. Moll and H.F. are each private individuals who indulge in moments of reflection, but each is also an urban dweller reliant on others and concerned for their welfare. Each is dependent on a world of shops, streets and trades. It is this interdependence of the private and the social which characterises Defoe's writing and makes him such a seminal figure in the history of the novel. For the first time we have a sense of London as a community, of man as a social being. The birth of the modern novel is signalled by two developments: the presentation of characters, and the detailed presentation of their environment. In Defoe we see for the first time the weaving together of these processes, the detailed depiction of the relationships between the individual and society.

In the chapters that follow it will be demonstrated how Defoe's diverse interests and skills combined to produce the earliest novels in English to embrace the modern world. First, his consuming interest in how people live: what he termed in the preface to *Moll Flanders* the 'incredible variety' of human life. His passionate interest in people – their occupations, homes and attitudes – enabled him to depict a rich variety of individuals and place them in a realistic and recognisable setting.

Secondly, his concern for facts. As a tradesman he was deeply interested in facts and statistics and he understood the realities that lay behind them; as a writer he possessed the gift of presenting those facts in human terms. *A Journal of the Plague Year* and *A Tour through the Whole Island* are interwoven with facts on all manner of topics presented in a way which enriches rather than deadens the narrative. Our understanding of what life was like for ordinary people in eighteenth-century England is greatly deepened by his skilful and homely use of realistic detail.

Thirdly, his conception of life as a journey. His own life had been one of movement not simply in a geographical sense but through a diverse range of occupations and experiences. When he came to distil his impressions in his major fictions he imbued his narratives with an exhilarating sense of movement: Singleton, Moll, Jack and Roxana are always journeying onwards in their quest for fulfilment. This sense of life as an adventure is in sharp contrast to the relatively static world of Bunyan. In place of a world that is preordained there is an impression of open-endedness, of a narrative in which anything is possible. The fate of Moll and Roxana are problematic to the end because Defoe knew in his bones that in this life nothing is fixed or final: all can change through the whim of chance or circumstance.

It is for these reasons – his concern for his characters both as individuals and citizens, his presentation of human life in its infinite variety, his passion for facts and awareness of the human condition as a journey in which nothing is predestined – that Defoe is regarded as the father of the modern novel. He brought to his writing an engaging sense of honesty, an instantly recognisable voice and an infectious sense of life's possibilities. Above all, he created in *Robinson Crusoe* and *Moll Flanders* the first novels in the English language and in doing so immeasurably enriched man's literary inheritance.

A Defoe Dictionary

Defoe was one of the most prolific writers in the English language, and a dictionary of his works would comprise a volume in itself. The dictionary which follows is an alphabetically arranged guide to those of his works which are primarily narrative in intention and are likely to be accessible to the reading public.

THE APPARITION OF MRS VEAL First published 1706. Full title: 'A True Relation of the Apparition of One Mrs Veal the Next Day After her Death, to One Mrs Bargrave at Canterbury, the 8th of September, 1705'. A short narrative which can be regarded as the first modern ghost story, 'Mrs Veal' is a circumstantial account of the visitation of a woman whose death has occurred the day prior to her alleged appearance.

CAPTAIN AVERY *See* THE KING OF PIRATES

CAPTAIN CARLETON First published 1728. Full title: *The Memoirs of an English Officer, Who served in the Dutch War of 1672, to the Peace of Utrecht. By Capt. George Carleton.* Fictitious military memoirs centred mainly in Holland and Spain in the early years of the eighteenth century.

CAPTAIN SINGLETON First published 4 June 1720. Full title: *The Life, Adventures and Piracies of the Famous Captain Singleton.* The autobiography of a waif who becomes an explorer and a pirate. The first half of the novel is a graphic account of a journey on foot across the mainland of Africa. This is followed by a vivid description of Singleton's career of piracy and adventure on the high seas.

COLONEL JACK First published December 1722. Full title: *The History and Remarkable Life of the Truly Honourable Colonel Jacque, Commonly called Colonel Jack.* The autobiography of an illegitimate child who, after a brief career as a thief, is kidnapped and transported to America where he becomes a farmer. Jack subsequently becomes a soldier and a trader, finally settling down in London to write his memoirs.

THE COMPLETE ENGLISH TRADESMAN   First published September 1725. Full title: *The Complete English Tradesman, In Familiar Letters, Directing him in all the several Parts and Progressions of Trade.* A compendium of practical advice for the aspiring tradesman. The book contains long narrative sections revealing Defoe's ascination with fictional techniques, particularly in Chapter 11: 'Of the Tradesman's Marrying Too Soon', and Chapter 15: 'Of Tradesmen Ruining One Another By Rumour and Clamour, By Scandal and Reproach'.

DUE PREPARATIONS FOR THE PLAGUE   First published 1722. Full title: *Due Preparations for the Plague, As Well for Soul as Body.* A practical handbook of advice and instruction in the face of bubonic plague, and an interesting anticipation of *A Journal of the Plague Year* published two months later. *Due Preparations* contains two narrative portions describing the impact of the plague on typical London families.

THE DUMB PHILOSOPHER   First published 1719. Full title: *The Dumb Philosopher; Or, Great Britain's Wonder.* A short narrative describing a mute who obtains the power of speech the day before his death and delivers an inspiring address relating the story of his life, and his religious beliefs.

DUNCAN CAMPBELL   First published 1720. Full title: *The History of the Life and Surprising Adventures of Mr Duncan Campbell.* The life and exploits of a Scottish clairvoyant during the years 1680–1712. The book offers an insight into Defoe's attitudes towards clairvoyance, dreams and the paranormal.

THE FORTUNATE MISTRESS   *See* ROXANA

THE FURTHER ADVENTURES OF ROBINSON CRUSOE   First published 1719. Full title: *The Further Adventures of Robinson Crusoe of York, Mariner.* A sequel to *Robinson Crusoe*, describing his subsequent adventures on the island and on the high seas.

A GENERAL HISTORY OF THE PIRATES   First published 1724 (volume 1), 1728 (volume 2). Full title: *A General History of the Robberies and Murders of the Most Notorious Pirates.* A compendium of biographies of eighteenth-century pirates, purportedly compiled by a

'Captain Charles Johnson'. The compilation includes biographies of the following pirates :

Volume One:
1. Henry Avery
2. John Martel
3. Edward Teach, alias Blackbeard
4. Stede Bonnet
5. Edward England
6. Charles Vane
7. John Rackam, Mary Read, Anne Bonny
8. Howel Davis
9. Bartholomew Roberts
10. Thomas Anstis
11. Richard Worley
12. George Lowther
13. Edward Low
14. John Evans
15. John Phillips
16. Francis Spriggs
17. John Smith, alias Gow

Volume Two:
1. Captain Misson
2. Thomas Tew
3. William Kid
4. John Bowen
5. John Halsey
6. Thomas White
7. Thomas Howard
8. David Williams
9. Samuel Burgess
10. Nathaniel North
11. Nathaniel North (continued)
12. Captain Condent
13. Captain Bellamy
14. Captain Lewis
15. John Cornelius
16. William Fly

JOHN GOW   First published 1725. Full title: *An Account of the Conduct and Proceedings of the late John Gow, alias Smith, Captain of the late Pirates.* A factual account of the piratical career of John Gow, his capture, trial and execution, narrated in Defoe's distinctive style.

JONATHAN WILD   First published 1725. Full title: *The True, Genuine and Perfect Account of the Life and Actions of Jonathan Wild.* An account of the life and career of an infamous fence and informer.

A JOURNAL OF THE PLAGUE YEAR   First published April 1722. Full title: *A Journal of the Plague Year, being Observations or Memorials of the most Remarkable Occurrences, as well Public as Private, which happened in London during the last Great Visitation in 1665.* The journal purports to be the diary of H.F., a saddler who lived in London during the bubonic plague.

THE KING OF PIRATES   First published 1719. Full title: *The King of Pirates: Being an account of the Famous Enterprises of Captain Avery, the Mock King of Madagascar.* An account of the piratical career of John Avery, told in the form of two letters allegedly written by Avery.

THE LIFE OF JOHN SHEPPARD   First published 1724. Full title: *The History of the Remarkable Life of John Sheppard.* An account of the life and career of a notorious criminal, published at a time when Sheppard's name was a household word due to his effrontery as a burglar and thief.

MADAGASCAR   *See* ROBERT DRURY'S JOURNAL

MEMOIRS OF A CAVALIER   First published 1720. Full title: *Memoirs of a Cavalier, or a Military Journal of the Wars in Germany, and the Wars in England, From the year 1632 to the year 1648.* A fictionalised history compiled by Defoe largely from published sources, describing the military adventures of a Colonel Andrew Newport during the Thirty Years War in Germany and the English Civil War.

MOLL FLANDERS   First published 27 January 1722. Full title: *The Fortunes and Misfortunes of the Famous Moll Flanders.* The fictional autobiography of a thief and woman of fortune who, after a long criminal career, repents of her past misdeeds and finds contentment and prosperity in marriage.

MRS VEAL *See* THE APPARITION OF MRS VEAL

A NEW VOYAGE ROUND THE WORLD   First published 1724. Full title: *A New Voyage Round the World, By a Course Never Sailed Before.* A realistic tale of adventures on land and sea told by an unnamed narrator who sails from England round the world between 1713 and 1717. This was the last imaginative story of its kind that Defoe wrote.

THE PIRATE GOW *See* JOHN GOW

ROBERT DRURY'S JOURNAL   First published 1729. Full title: *Madagascar; Or, Robert Drury's Journal.* The fictional autobiography of an adventurer in Madagascar during the early years of the eighteenth century.

ROBINSON CRUSOE   First published 25 April 1719. Full title: *The Life and Strange Surprising Adventures of Robinson Crusoe of York, Mariner.* The fictional account of a young Englishman who is shipwrecked on an uninhabited island off the coast of South America, where he lives for 27 years. The story is based in part on the experiences of Alexander Selkirk, a Scot who was marooned on the island of Juan Fernandez for four years (1704–9). *Robinson Crusoe* has been translated into almost every language and has even become the basis of pantomime.

ROXANA   First published 1724. Full title: *Roxana, The Fortunate Mistress.* The fictional autobiography of a courtesan and adventuress, the daughter of Huguenot parents who settled in England. *Roxana* makes extensive use of flashback and reveals Defoe's growing mastery of the craft of the novel.

A TOUR THROUGH THE WHOLE ISLAND OF GREAT BRITAIN   First published 1724–6. Full title: *A Tour Through the whole Island of Great Britain, Divided into Circuits or Journies, giving A Particular and Diverting Account of Whatever is Curious and worth Observation.* An account of Defoe's journeys through England and Scotland on horseback, revealing his imaginative response to the emerging modern world.

Key to the Characters and Locations

This section consists of an alphabetically arranged dictionary of the characters and places having a significant role in Defoe's fiction.

The following abbreviations are used throughout:

Cavalier	*Memoirs of a Cavalier*
Crusoe	*Robinson Crusoe*
Jack	*Colonel Jack*
Journal	*A Journal of the Plague Year*
Moll	*Moll Flanders*
Roxana	*Roxana, The Fortunate Mistress*
Singleton	*Captain Singleton*
Veal	'A True Relation of the Apparition of one Mrs Veal'

AFRICA.   The scene of Singleton's epic journey from the east to the west coast. In describing the journey across the then unknown continent Defoe anticipated many of Stanley's discoveries, in particular the three great lakes of Tanganyika, Victoria and Nyasa; the source of the Nile; and the course of the river Congo. For many years his narrative was assumed to be an account of an actual journey.   *Singleton*

ALDGATE.   A district of East London, near Whitechapel, in Defoe's time a thriving commercial area. H.F., the narrator of *Journal*, lives 'about mid-way between Aldgate Church and Whitechapel Bars, on the left hand or North side of the street'.   *Journal*

AMY.   Roxana's faithful maid. Resolute, shrewd and practical, Amy accompanies her mistress through the vicissitudes of her career, abetting and counselling her. When Roxana returns to London at the age of 35, Amy is sent by her mistress to discover the whereabouts of her children, for she is the only person who can be trusted with such a commission. It is Amy who discovers that

Roxana's eldest daughter Susan is employed in their own house. Amy assists Roxana to hide from her daughter but Susan pursues them implacably. *Roxana*

AVERY, CAPTAIN JOHN.   A real pirate who is the subject of Defoe's semi-fictitious account *The King of Pirates* (1719). The pamphlet purports to be a narrative written by Avery himself, explaining and justifying his actions. Avery reappears in *Singleton*, where the hero joins forces temporarily with the pirate colony set up by Avery on the shore of Africa.

BANKER, THE.   The fifth husband of Moll Flanders. They marry at Brickhill and live happily together for five years, she bearing him two children. She says of him: 'I lived with this husband in the utmost tranquillity; he was a quiet, sensible, sober man, virtuous, modest, sincere, and in his business diligent and just.' After one of his clerks steals a large sum of money from the bank he is overcome with worry and finally dies. *Moll*

BARGRAVE, MRS.   A lady of good character and cheerful disposition, she lives alone in Canterbury. One day her old friend Mrs Veal calls on her unexpectedly and the two hold a long conversation about former times. They also discuss matters of belief and the nature of life after death. Some days later Mrs Bargrave learns that Mrs Veal had died 24 hours before their meeting: she had therefore been talking to an apparition. *Veal*

BELEAU, MADEMOISELLE DE.   The real name of the lady who comes to be known as ROXANA (*q.v.*).

CAVALIER, THE.   Born in Shropshire in 1608, the son of a gentleman of fortune, he is convinced that 'the consequences of my life may allow me to suppose some extraordinary influence affected my birth'. After an Oxford education he decides to roam the world accompanied by a friend. He serves briefly in the French army and travels in Germany, taking part in the Thirty Years' War (1618–48) and distinguishing himself for bravery. Returning to England, he becomes embroiled in the Civil War (1641–8), fighting on behalf of the King. Following the defeat of the royal forces at the battle of Naseby, the Cavalier is content to end his military career, reflecting that 'for my part I went home fully contented, since I could do my royal master no better service'. *Cavalier*

CLEAVE, SIR WALTER. Usually referred to by Moll as 'the Bath gentleman'. His wife is in a mental institution, and after Moll has nursed him through an illness he and Moll become good friends. For two years they enjoy a chaste relationship, then she becomes his mistress. They live together illicitly for six years and she bears him a child. After a further bout of illness he casts her from his life. *Moll*

CRUSOE, ROBINSON. Born in York in 1632, the son of a German father and an English mother, his original surname is Kreutznaer but this is soon anglicised as Crusoe. Against his parents advice he insists on going to sea, being eager to see foreign lands. After many adventures he arrives in Brazil, where he invests in land and grows tobacco. Still smitten with wanderlust, he sets sail with thirteen other men in September 1659, but a storm blows them off course into the mouth of the River Orinoco (Venezuela). A second storm forces them to abandon ship and Crusoe alone succeeds in reaching land, an uninhabited island 50 miles southeast of Trinidad. For 23 years he lives alone on the island, constructing a home for himself and learning the skills of making bread, pottery, carpentry and husbandry. He keeps a journal and occupies his time in hunting for food, exploring the island, rearing goats and abortive attempts to construct a boat. One day he is surprised to see a naked footprint in the sand and is alarmed to reflect that he is no longer alone.

His years of solitude are ended when he rescues a savage trying to escape from cannibals from the mainland. Crusoe names the savage 'Friday' and adopts him as his servant and companion. Eventually the two are joined by a castaway Spaniard and another savage who proves to be Friday's father. When an English ship anchors off the island under the control of mutineers, Crusoe assists the captain to overthrow his captors. After 27 years of exile (not 28 as Defoe states on the title-page) he then leaves the island, embarking for England with Friday. He arrives in England in June 1686, to find his parents are both dead. After further travels to Portugal and France he returns to his homeland, where he settles and marries. Following the death of his wife he again has the urge to put to sea and revisits his island. Here he finds that the mutineers he had left behind have established a thriving colony.

Crusoe is characteristically English in his love of order and fairness. His story ends with the comments: 'I shared the island into parts with them, reserved to my self the property of the whole, but gave them such parts respectively as they agreed on.' To the end his concern is for the welfare of the island and its population, which he regards as his domain. *Crusoe*

DUTCH MERCHANT, THE. An honourable man who proposes marriage to Roxana. She at first declines him, fearing that marriage will deprive her of independence. Years later they meet again and she consents to marry him. She says of him: 'My new spouse and I lived a very regular contemplative life, and in itself a life filled with all humane felicity.' *Roxana*

FLANDERS, MOLL. Born in Newgate prison in 1613, the daughter of a convicted thief, Moll is cared for by gypsies and then abandoned when still a small child. She aspires to be a gentlewoman and a nurse teaches her the rudiments of gentility. Following the nurse's death Moll becomes a servant in the home of a wealthy family and is seduced at the age of eighteen by the eldest son. She marries the younger brother, Robin, and has two children by him. After five years of marriage Robin dies; Moll then marries a draper who flees to France to escape his creditors. Moll is forced into hiding and is eventually courted by a gentleman who marries her under the illusion that she is wealthy.

She and her new husband emigrate to Virginia and remain there for eight years, but she realises to her horror that he is in fact her half-brother. She separates from him and returns to England, taking up residence in Bath. Moll soon attracts the attention of a wealthy gentleman and becomes his mistress. After a six-year relationship they part, Moll pretending to be a woman of substance when in reality she has no means.

She moves to Lancashire and there meets an Irish lord, Jemy, with whom she falls genuinely in love. She marries him only to discover that he has no money; each has deceived the other. He leaves her to pursue his own destiny and she returns to London, marrying again (for the last time). Her fifth husband is a banker, to whom she is contentedly married for five years.

After the death of the banker Moll becomes bankrupt and embarks on a career of theft. For ten years she is a shoplifter and pickpocket, living under a series of false names and disguises. She also earns money from prostitution. At the age of 60 she is arrested and committed to Newgate, where she repents of her past misdeeds. She is sentenced to death but the sentence is commuted to transportation, in view of her apparently genuine remorse. Her former husband Jemy, committed for highway robbery, is transported at the same time. Together they sail to America and settle in Maryland, where they prosper. After eight years in America Moll and Jemy return to England, where they resolve 'to spend the remainder of our years in sincere penitence, for the wicked lives we have lived.' *Moll*

FRIDAY, MAN. A young black man rescued from cannibals by Crusoe and adopted as his companion. He was 'a comely handsome fellow, perfectly well made; with straight strong limbs, not too large; tall and well shaped, and as I reckon, about twenty six years of age'. Crusoe teaches him to speak English, to wear clothes, and the rudiments of religion and civilisation. Eventually they are joined by Friday's father who is overjoyed to be reunited with his son. After five years together on the island, when Friday proves himself to be utterly devoted to his rescuer, Crusoe embarks with him for England. Friday remains with Crusoe during his subsequent travels in Europe. *Crusoe*

H.F.. A saddler who lives in Whitechapel, London, during the Great Plague of 1665. When the news of the epidemic first reaches him he wishes to flee, and is urged to do so by his elder brother. All his attempts to escape are frustrated, and H.F. interprets his failure as a sign from God that he should remain in London and look after his business. H.F. is unmarried but he employs a number of servants and has a house and a warehouse in addition to his shop. He rejects astrological and supernatural explanations of the plague and is convinced that the disease has a rational cause.

He gives a graphic account of the spread of the plague, visiting a burial pit at Aldgate and describing scenes of death, looting and drunkenness. At its height the epidemic reaches crisis proportions, many people fleeing from their homes and others committing suicide or becoming delirious. When the plague begins to subside, life slowly returns to normality and those who have escaped return gratefully to their homes. H.F. is a calm, methodical observer of terrible scenes and seeks to present an accurate, meticulous account based on his personal observation and on published reports. *Journal*

HEATH, DOCTOR.　A London physician and a close friend of H.F., the narrator of *Journal*. Heath is described as 'a good Christian, as well as a good physician: his agreeable conversation was a very great support to me in the worst of this terrible time'. Heath persuades H.F. to abandon his practice of wandering the streets and instead to confine himself indoors until the epidemic has abated. H.F. tries to follow his friend's advice but finds it is not practicable 'as I had not laid in a store of provision for such a retreat'. *Journal*

HUMPHRY.　The third husband of Moll Flanders. He originally courts her under the illusion that she possesses a fortune and is chagrined to learn that she is poor. He and Moll emigrate to Virginia but she realises that they have married illegally: he is in fact her half-brother. They have a son, also named Humphry, whom she meets again many years later. Husband and wife become estranged, and after eight years in Virginia Moll returns to England without him. *Moll*

JACK, CAPTAIN.　Colonel Jack's boyhood companion and the son of his nurse. He is 'a squat, big, strong made boy... brutish, bloody, and cruel in his disposition'. He participates in many of Jack's adventures as a pickpocket and is eventually executed for highway robbery. *Jack*

JACK, COLONEL.　Jack describes himself as 'a poor unhappy tractable dog, willing enough, and capable too, to learn anything, if he had had any but the devil for his schoolmaster... I passed among my comrades for a bold resolute boy.' An illegitimate child, he is entrusted to a nurse who is urged to bring him up as a gentleman. After the nurse's death Jack falls in with a gang of pickpockets and embarks on a career of thieving. His associates feel no compunction at their actions but Jack feels guilty, particularly when an old woman is robbed. When the leader of the gang is hanged Jack travels to Scotland and is taught to read and write by a scholar. He enlists in the army but then deserts and flees to Newcastle, where he is duped and carried aboard ship. The ship is bound for Virginia, where he is to be sold as a servant. He proves himself a good worker and is promoted to be an overseer, eventually prospering as a farmer. After twelve years he returns to England, where he is tricked into marriage with an extravagant wife.

Jack divorces her and enlists as a soldier in the service of the king of France. He takes part in military campaigns in Italy and, after involvement in many colourful adventures, returns to England where he lives quietly under a pseudonym. After another unfortunate marriage he finds happiness with Margaret, a plain but dutiful servant girl. When she dies in childbirth Jack returns to Virginia, where he finds he is a man of substance because of his flourishing estate. Here he meets again his divorced first wife and marries her. His past military escapades catch up with him and for a time he is a wanted man, forced into hiding in the West Indies. After being pardoned by King George, he embarks on a lucrative career trading in contraband. He ends his narrative by reflecting on his misspent life, convinced that 'an invisible over-ruling power, a hand influenced from above, governs all our actions of every kind'. *Jack*

JEMY.   The fourth husband of Moll Flanders, who usually referred to him as 'my Lancashire husband'. Though she is genuinely in love with him they marry under false pretences, each being convinced that the other is wealthy. After only seven months of marriage they separate, Moll returning to London and Jemy deserting her to become a highwayman. Years later when Moll is committed to Newgate prison for theft she learns that Jemy is in the same prison for highway robbery. The two are transported to America. After an absence of eight years they return to England where they intend to spend the remainder of their lives. She remarks of him: 'I loved my Lancashire husband entirely, as indeed I have ever done from the beginning.' *Moll*

JOHN.   A biscuit baker from Wapping, formerly a soldier. Together with his brother Thomas and a friend, Richard, he succeeds in escaping from London during the Great Plague and camps in the countryside near Epping until the epidemic is over. *Journal* (*See also* THOMAS)

JUAN FERNANDEZ.   A group of three islands situated in the Pacific

Ocean 350 miles off Valparaiso, Chile. On the largest of these, Mas a Tierra, Alexander Selkirk was marooned from October 1704 to February 1709. An account of his experiences was subsequently included in Woodes Rogers's *Cruising Voyage Round the World* (1712). This account was known to Defoe, who may also have met and interviewed Selkirk. Defoe used some of the details of the island in describing Crusoe's domain. He also used the fact that Selkirk had worn a coat and cap made from goat-skins. *Crusoe*

KNOX, ROBERT. A sailor whose account of his adventures is interpolated into *Singleton* (pp. 238–49). Knox was a real person (1640–1720), who was captured by natives of Ceylon and held prisoner for nineteen years. On his release he entered the service of the East India Company and wrote the first account of Ceylon in English.

LINEN DRAPER, THE. Moll Flanders's second husband. She is attracted to the idea of marrying a tradesman, provided he is a man of substance: 'I was not averse to a tradesman, but then I would have a tradesman forsooth that was something of a gentleman too.' He lives extravagantly, squandering his money on travel and possessions until he is obliged to flee to France to escape his creditors, leaving her in straitened circumstances.   *Moll*

LONDON. Defoe knew London extremely well. His childhood was spent in the parish of St Stephen, Coleman Street (in the City), and after his marriage his business premises were situated nearby at Freemans Yard, Cornhill.

Many of the scenes depicted in *Moll* take place in London, although G. A. Starr comments that 'much of her path...was obliterated when Smithfield market was expanded in the 19th century'. Many of her exploits take place in the area around Newgate Street, the City of London, which was at that time a tortuous maze of alleys and courtyards.

Journal contains numerous references to London and its surrounding area. A detailed commentary on the topographical references in *Journal* can be found on pp. 292–9 of the World's Classics edition (Oxford University Press).

The boyhood adventures described in the early pages of *Jack* take place in and about Stepney.

See also ALDGATE, MINORIES, NEWGATE, SPITALFIELDS, STEPNEY

MARGARET ('MOGGY'). A plain but conscientious servant girl to whom Colonel Jack proposes marriage. She befriends his children from an earlier marriage and is 'always helpful in directing and ordering things for them, and mighty handy about them'. She and Jack are happily married for four years but she dies in childbirth after an outbreak of smallpox. *Jack*

MINORIES, THE. An area of London adjacent to the Tower. It is in a courtyard in the Minories that Roxana goes into hiding when being sought by her daughter: 'I was now in a perfect retreat indeed; remote from the eyes of all that ever had seen me.' *Roxana*

NEWGATE. Once the principal London prison, it stood at the corner of Old Bailey and was damaged but not destroyed in the Great Fire. Defoe was briefly imprisoned here (May 1703), accused of writing a seditious libel 'The Shortest Way with the Dissenters'. The prison was demolished in 1777. Moll Flanders was born here in 1613 and 60 years later was confined to the prison for fifteen weeks while awaiting transportation. *Moll*

ORINOCO. A river flowing northwards through Venezuela (spelt 'Oroonoque' by Defoe), the mouth of which is the supposed location of Crusoe's island. *Crusoe*
(*See also* JUAN FERNANDEZ)

QUAKERESS, THE. A 'most pleasant and agreeable lady' with whom Roxana and her maid live in retirement while in hiding. She is described as having had 'a full share of good breeding, sufficient to her if she had been a duchess'. *Roxana*

RICHARD. A joiner living at Shadwell, near Wapping. When he learns that two brothers are planning to leave London during the plague and seek sanctuary in the countryside he joins forces with them. He is described as having 'no wealth but his box or basket of tools, with the help of which he could at any time get his living.' *Journal*
(*See also* THOMAS)

ROBIN. Moll Flanders's first husband and the younger brother of her seducer. She consents to marry him, though in reality she loves his brother. Following Robin's death after five years of marriage she is left with two children whom she leaves with her inlaws. *Moll*

ROBIN. An experienced pickpocket who befriends Colonel Jack and initiates him into crime. *Jack*
(*See also* WILL)

ROXANA. Born in France of Huguenot parents who settle in England, Roxana is beautiful, vain and ambitious, but is trapped into an unfortunate marriage at the age of fifteen. Her husband proves to be a wastrel who dissipates her money and abandons her with a young family. Together with her faithful maid Amy she moves to Paris, leaving her children in the care of relatives. She becomes the mistress of a prince for eight years, travelling in Italy and France and bearing him two sons. Roxana returns to England but is forced into hiding when accused of handling stolen jewellery. For some years she is a wealthy courtesan, pursuing a career of 'prosperous wickedness' in the course of which she becomes the mistress of royalty. Amy discovers that Roxana's eldest daughter Susan is working in their own kitchen as a maid; she does not wish to reveal her identity to Susan as she is smitten with remorse for her misspent life. Roxana and Amy change lodgings but Susan learns of their whereabouts and pursues them relentlessly.

Unscrupulous and amoral, Roxana ends her story inconclusively, telling the reader: 'I fell into a dreadful course of calamities, and Amy also; the very reverse of our former good days.' *Roxana*

SINGLETON BOB (CAPTAIN). A waif who knows nothing of his parents, Singleton is kidnapped when still a small child and sold to a gypsy. After the death of the gypsy a ship's captain takes a liking to him and takes him on several voyages to Newfoundland. The ship is captured by pirates and Bob becomes the servant of a Portuguese sailor. After many adventures at sea in which he becomes hardened to theft and profligacy he is marooned on the coast of Madagascar, where he is joined by 27 other sailors. They succeed in reaching the mainland of Africa and decide to try to reach the west coast at Angola, an overland journey of at least 2000 miles. Singleton eventually reaches his goal and returns to

England, where he soon squanders his money. He embarks on a career of piracy in the West Indies, taking prisoner a Quaker named William Walters who soon proves to be a friend and ally. The pirates voyage to Africa and India in search of wealth and adventure, amassing a considerable fortune. At length Singleton wearies of his criminal life and settles in England, marrying Walters's sister. He confides that in his life of respectability he is much more happy than he deserves.

Singleton is characteristic of Defoe's narrators in his preoccupation with criminality and repentance. In common with Moll, Jack and Roxana, he looks back on a long life of picaresque adventures, seeking to learn what lessons he can from his amoral career and confides his experiences to other. His narrative is given added verisimilitude by its inclusion of real people, notably Captain Avery and Robert Knox. *Singleton*

SMITH. A wealthy Virginia planter who becomes Jack's employer when the latter is sold into servitude. He is described as 'a great man in the country, and a Justice of the Peace'. Jack is a model worker and Smith promotes him to be an overseer. Jack cannot bring himself to whip the negro slaves and is resented by the other overseers, who accuse him of being too lenient. Eventually Smith is convinced of the wisdom of Jack's attitude and is won over to a more humane regime. Smith sets Jack up as a farmer and builds a house for him. He offers to release his employee from his servitude but Jack insists on remaining in his service. *Jack*

SPITALFIELDS. An area of East London (now part of Stepney), formerly a centre for Huguenot refugees. Defoe knew the district well, for it was here that he lay in hiding after the publication of *The Shortest Way*. Roxana leaves her five children in the care of relations at Spitalfields. *Roxana*

STEPNEY. A district of East London, the scene of Jack's boyhood. Goodman's fields, where he was brought up, was in Defoe's time an open area near the Tower of London. *Jack*

SUSAN. Roxana's eldest daughter. Left in the care of relatives at Spitalfields, she finds employment as a kitchen maid and eventually takes a post working in the household of her own mother. Roxana does not wish to identify herself to Susan, for she is ashamed of her amoral life. Roxana changes her address but Susan suspecting her identity, pursues her from one hiding place to another. 'She haunted me like an evil spirit', says her mother, 'as if, like a hound, she had a hot scent.' The story ends inconclusively, the reader being left to infer that Susan has been murdered by Roxana's maid, Amy. *Roxana*

THOMAS. A sailmaker from Wapping, formerly a sailor. Together with his brother John and a friend, Richard, they consider what action they should take when the plague of 1665 breaks out. Thomas wishes to remain where he is but John is in favour of moving. After debating both sides of the question they decide to leave their homes and attempt to escape from the infected areas. They are joined by thirteen others, also fleeing from the plague. Barred from passing through Walthamstow (the local people fear they are contagious), they make their way towards Epping, where they encamp. The villagers supply them with food until the plague subsides and they can return home. The narrator remarks that 'their story has a moral in every part of it, and their whole conduct...is a pattern for all poor men to follow'. *Journal*

VEAL, MRS. A 'gentlewoman of about thirty years of age...a very pious woman', she keeps house for her brother in Dover. One day she visits her old friend Mrs Bargrave and the two hold a lengthy conversation. Some days later Mrs Bargrave learns that Mrs Veal had died precisely twenty four hours before their meeting. *Veal*

VIRGINIA. Moll Flanders and her husband, Humphry, emigrate to Virginia where they live on a plantation with her mother in law. Many years later, by which time she has married again, Moll is transported to Virginia and discovers that her former husband and their son are still living. She has an emotional reunion with her son at Chesapeake Bay. *Moll*

Jack is sold as a servant on a Virginia plantation and eventually prospers there as a farmer. He returns to Virginia with his son years later and finds his estate is flourishing. *Jack*

WALTERS, WILLIAM. A Quaker surgeon who becomes Singleton's ally and confidant. He is described as 'a comic fellow indeed, a man of very good solid sense, and an excellent surgeon; but what was worth all, very good humoured and pleasant in his conversation, and a bold, stout, brave fellow'. While on a Spanish ship en route for Barbados he is captured by Singleton and soon impresses his captors with his bravery and wisdom. Gradually Walters becomes Singleton's principal adviser, demonstrating his calmness and rationality at times of crisis, and urging the pirate to abandon his criminal career. The two friends travel to Venice incognito, planning to settle in England where Walters's relatives are still living. Finally Singleton and Walters realise their ambition, Singleton marrying Walters's widowed sister.

Defoe took great pains to make the character as lifelike as possible, interpolating long passages of dialogue in which the Quaker reveals his sensitivity and dry sense of humour.   *Singleton*

WILL.   An experienced pickpocket who befriends Colonel Jack and initiates him into a career as a thief. He aspires to be a gentleman and becomes a proficient thief and burglar in his quest for riches. He and his accomplices break into a house and kill the gardener; Will is arrested and hanged. (Note that the character is first named 'Robin' and later becomes 'Will': an inadvertence on Defoe's part.) *Jack*

Part II

The Shorter Fiction

Defoe turned to the writing of fiction after a long apprenticeship in journalism. Before the publication of *The Life and Strange Surprising Adventures of Robinson Crusoe* in 1719 he had written pamphlets, verse, political satire and religious polemic in addition to writing and editing regular issues of *The Review*. The latter occasionally included short stories and sketches in which he would insert dialogues between imaginary correspondents or comment on the political and religious controversies of the day. This journalism, together with such satirical pieces as *The Shortest Way with the Dissenters* (1702) and *And What if the Pretender Should Come?*(1713) proved to be a most valuable training in literary expression. For through the medium of these articles, pamphlets and stories he was gaining experience in the adoption of a *persona* other than himself and acquiring the narrative skills that were later to flower so impressively in *Moll Flanders* and *A Journal of the Plague Year*. In 1705 he published *The Consolidator; Or, Memoirs of Sundry Transactions from the World in the Moon*, an account of an imaginary voyage to a lunar kingdom. This is a laboured allegory on contemporary English institutions and politicians, an allegory which may well have been the inspiration behind Swift's *Gulliver's Travels* (1726). Though much of the fiction of this period seems heavy-handed and prolix to a modern reader it is salutory to remind ourselves that throughout a period of twenty years (1700–20) Defoe was continually shaping and refining a literary style that was to make him one of the foremost writers of his day. No writer could produce such a volume of work of such diversity and over two decades without gaining an insight into literary techniques and a growing self-confidence in the handling of dialogue and incident.

Short pieces by Defoe, for example 'The Ghost of Dorothy Dingley' and 'In Defence of his Right', are occasionally included in anthologies of short stories, but these are not so much short stories as fragments selected from longer works. Extracts from *Robinson Crusoe* and *Moll Flanders* are sometimes anthologised in the same way. These are certainly striking examples of his prose style but do not conform to the classic definition of the short story laid down by Edgar Allan Poe that 'in the whole composition there should be no word written of which the tendency, direct or indirect, is not to the one pre-established design'.[29] However, Defoe certainly published one story which fully conforms to this criteria and which has exerted a profound influence on the short story in English. This tale merits close attention as a case study in the art of fiction.

'A True Relation of the Apparition of one Mrs Veal' was published in 1706, when Defoe was 46. It merits an important place in the history of English literature as the first 'modern' ghost story and the earliest of Defoe's allegedly 'true' works of fiction. It is a short story of some 4000 words, written in his characteristic style of circumstantial reportage in which he took care to achieve a feeling of authenticity. In common with many distinguished short stories its basic plot is a simple one: a Mrs Bargrave has a long conversation in her home with an old friend, Mrs Veal, only to discover later that Mrs Veal had died exactly 24 hours before this encounter. The reader is therefore faced with the notion that if the conversation was real and not imaginary the lady encountered by Mrs Bargrave was an apparition. What elevates the story above so much gothic writing of the period is Defoe's skill in narrating it in a vividly journalistic style, his mastery of construction and the deftness with which he establishes the reliability of the principal witness. So convincing is his technique that the reader willingly suspends disbelief. The story is well constructed and demonstrates that the years of experience Defoe had gained in pamphleteering and in writing and editing *The Review* had helped to fashion an impressive self-confidence in the handling of literary material. 'Mrs Veal' is a fascinating case-study in the art of the storyteller.

The introductory paragraph describing Mrs Bargrave is followed by a paragraph summarising the life and background of Mrs Veal. We learn that Mrs Veal was 'a gentlewoman of about thirty years of age', that she was a very pious woman and for some years had been troubled with fits. This is followed by an account of her friendship with Mrs Bargrave. These opening passages then lead into the core of the narrative: the circumstantial description of the apparition and its aftermath. The story is rounded off with an eloquent conclusion reaffirming Mrs Bargrave's trustworthiness and refuting the scepticism of those who doubt her statement. The structure has become the classic pattern for short narratives of this kind and has been widely emulated. Poe, in 'A Tale of the Ragged Mountains' and 'The Gold-Bug', and Wells, in 'The Plattner Story' and 'The Queer Story of Brownlow's Newspaper', employ a similar technique. All four narratives depend for much of their effect on some or all of the following elements: an outer narrator who relates an apparently fantastic story with an air of sober realism, the careful accumulation of circumstantial detail, the skilful pacing of incident, and a fluent documentary style.

The first point to notice about the story is that, in common with many of the tales of Poe and Wells, it is not told in the first person but by an 'outer narrator'. It would have been entirely possible for Defoe to have told the story in the first person as if written by Mrs Bargrave; given his propensity towards autobiographical narratives this would probably have been his natural inclination. It would have added a dimension of immediacy to her account but there would remain a doubt in the reader's mind as to her credibility. Instead, the story is told by a Justice of the Peace known personally to Mrs Bargrave, writing to a friend in London. The effect of this is twofold: to distance the narrator by filtering the account through his rather dry, legal mind (a similar technique is employed in Stevenson's *The Master of Ballantrae*), and to provide an independent person who can vouch for Mrs Bargrave's integrity. The device greatly enhances the impact of the story and heightens the impression of factuality.

Consider, for example, the effect achieved by the opening paragraph:

> This thing is so rare in all its circumstances and on so good authority, that my reading and conversation has not given me anything like it. It is fit to gratify the most ingenious and serious inquirer. Mrs Bargrave is the person to whom Mrs Veal appeared after her death; she is my intimate friend, and I can vouch for her reputation for these last fifteen or sixteen years, on my own knowledge; and I can confirm the good character she had from her youth to the time of my acquaintance.

This introduction establishes a number of pertinent facts: that the narrative is 'rare in all its circumstances'; that its truth is asserted by a most reliable witness; that Mrs Bargrave is an 'intimate friend' of the narrator. The opening prepares the reader to anticipate an unusual tale, for the storyteller claims that 'my reading and conversation has not given me anything like it'. The language is calm and matter of fact, precisely what one would expect from a magistrate accustomed to handling data in a judicial manner. The tone is finely attuned to achieve the effect Defoe has in mind: to convince his readers that he is describing events that have actually occurred, that is, that Mrs Bargrave actually saw and conversed with Mrs Veal on the day following her death.

Defoe was a trained journalist who had acquired considerable skill in the composition of vividly written accounts of apparently real events. The following passage is an interesting example of his technique :

> In this house, on the eighth of September last, viz, 1705, she was sitting alone in the forenoon, thinking over her unfortunate life, and arguing herself into a due resignation to Providence, though her condition seemed hard: 'And,' said she, 'I have been provided for hitherto, and doubt not but I shall be still, and am well satisfied that my afflictions shall end when it is most fit for me.' And then took up her sewing work, which she had no sooner done but she hears a knocking at the door; she went to see who it was there, and this proved to be Mrs Veal, her old friend, who was in a riding-habit. At that moment of time the clock struck twelve at noon.

One notes the precise detail of time and place; 'on the 8th of September last', 'the clock struck twelve at noon'. There is the confirmatory detail that Mrs Bargrave is sitting alone and that she has taken up her sewing. Not content with describing the external details of her stance and occupation, the narrator tells us the thoughts passing through her mind: she is 'thinking over her unfortunate life' and reflecting on the vagaries of providence. When Mrs Veal knocks at the door Defoe adds the characteristic touch that she was 'in a riding-habit'. The fact that the clock strikes at the instant of her appearance fixes her in the reader's mind, as does her statement that she is feeling unwell and had a strong desire to see her old friend before going on a journey.

Throughout their conversation (the two ladies are together for an hour and three-quarters) there is a steady reiteration of circumstantial detail. They discuss family matters, reminisce about the past, and engage in a long discussion concerning the books they have read in times of adversity. This leads on to a discussion about faith, and life after death. A number of details of the encounter remain firmly in Mrs Bargrave's memory: the fact that Mrs Veal asks her to write a letter to her brother, that she mentions various bequests of rings and gold coins, that she expresses a wish to see Mrs Bargrave's daughter. Particularly striking is Mrs Bargrave's insistence that she actually felt her visitor's clothes:

> And to divert Mrs Veal, as she thought, she took hold of her gown-sleeve several times, and commended it. Mrs Veal told her it was a scoured silk, and newly made up.

The detail is of more than passing significance for it transpires that only Mrs Veal and her dressmaker knew that the gown was scoured: the fact that Mrs Bargrave clearly recalls the texture of the garment strengthens her veracity in the eyes of her neighbours. But the detail adds solidity to Mrs Bargrave's account – Mrs Veal was not only seen and heard, but *touched*. One recalls the description of the artificial diamond in Wells's short story 'The Diamond Maker': 'Leaning forward towards the gas-lamp, I tried the thing on my watch-glass, and scored a white line across that with the greatest ease.'[30] The reader does not doubt the reality of the diamond, any more than he questions the reality of Mrs Veal: the fact that her friend actually feels the gown, not once but several times, seems incontrovertible. There are the additional facts that Mrs Veal complains of feeling unwell; that she sits in an elbow-chair to 'keep her from falling on either side'; and that she is most insistent on Mrs Bargrave writing a letter on her behalf. All this seems to confirm the impression of a real, living presence: there is nothing ghostly about her whatever.

The repeated references to time serve as a reminder of mortality: 'At that moment of time the clock struck twelve at noon'; 'it cannot be thought that an hour and three quarters' conversation could all be retained'; 'a turning interrupted the sight of her, which was three quarters after one in the afternoon'. Time is, of course, an important element in the story, for everything hinges on the revelation that Mrs Veal has died the day preceding her supposed conversation with Mrs Bargrave, at precisely the same hour. But the frequent references to the passage of time serve an additional function as a reminder of the transience of earthly life. Mrs Veal's insistence that she is about to embark on a journey – a fact which is mentioned several times, her preoccupation with death, her repeated references to the hereafter, her evident haste to depart, all strengthen the impression of a character who is well aware of her mortality and anxious to impress this fact on her friend. When she begs Mrs Bargrave to pass on to her brother an account of their conversation she is most insistent that this is done: 'though it seems impertinent to you now, you will see more reason for it hereafter'. With a sure instinct for dramatic effect Defoe announces the fact of Mrs Veal's death midway through his story rather than at the end, and in the driest of language:

> Mrs Veal died the seventh of September, at twelve o'clock at noon, of her fits, and had not above four hours' senses before her death, in which time she received the sacrament.

All along the reader has been aware that the encounter took place on 8 September. What then is the explanation for the apparent contradiction? Defoe insists in his Preface that 'This relation is matter of fact, and attended with such circumstances as may induce any reasonable man to believe it.' We know now that Mrs Veal and Mrs Bargrave actually existed, and that in writing his short story he was giving fictional expression to events that, to the best of his belief, were true.

But even if this were not so, the story stands or falls on its *literary* merits. Defoe was surely right to conclude his account with the observation: 'And why we should dispute matter of fact, because we cannot solve things of which we can have no certain or demonstrative notions, seems strange to me.' Such agnosticism will strike an answering chord with many readers, but it is important to remind ourselves that it was written at a time of religious piety when faith was the norm, not the exception. 'A True Relation of the Apparition of one Mrs Veal' implicitly questions the concept of absolute certainty, and posits instead the notion that some things are unknown and apparently unknowable.

The story has been described as 'a classic example of how to invest the supernatural with complete credibility'.[31] In its sober style, its pacing, its careful use of detail and marshalling of corroborative evidence it anticipates the work of M. R. James and Algernon Blackwood. At the same time it can be regarded as a pioneering exercise in the vein of brilliantly sustained realism exemplified in the short stories of Poe and Wells. The writer of 'Mrs Veal' was the same man who, a few years later, would astonish the world with *Robinson Crusoe*.

Robinson Crusoe

Robinson Crusoe occupies an important place in literary history as the first English novel and the forerunner of the realist tradition continued by Fielding and Dickens. There had, of course, been works of fiction prior to 1719 but these were not *novels* as we would recognise them today. What was new about Defoe's narrative was its convincing air of verisimilitude and the fact that its central character is a solid, believable individual with an inner life of remarkable consistency and power. Defoe himself draws attention to its verisimilitude in the Preface when he remarks: 'The Editor believes the thing to be a just History of Fact; neither is there any Appearance of Fiction in it.' The story has exercised a continuing hold on the human imagination; it has been translated into almost every language on earth and has even formed the basis of pantomime. Clearly, a story that has achieved the status of a fable must possess considerable literary and imaginative qualities and respond to some deep need in the human psyche. *Robinson Crusoe* is in fact one of the great myths of Western civilisation, entertaining succeeding generations with its vision of a solitary Englishman on a desert island laboriously rebuilding a semblance of order around his lonely domain. As a 'desert island' myth the novel has spawned a multitude of imitations ranging from Ballantyne's *The Coral Island* (1857) to Golding's *The Lord of the Flies* (1954) and exercises an enduring fascination as a case study in survival.[32] Today we no longer read the novel as a child's adventure story or a religious parable, but recognise it as a watershed in English literature and an allegory of the human condition.

The narrative owes much of its impact to its air of immediacy, to the reader's sense that the events are happening as Crusoe writes them down. This is partly a matter of the first-person narration and Defoe's intensely personal style. There are numerous asides in which the narrator addresses the reader directly – 'As I have troubled you with none of my Sea-Journals, so I shall trouble you now with none of my Land-Journal' (p. 289); 'Be pleas'd to take a Sketch of my Figure as follows' (p. 149); 'as you will see presently' (p. 250). As the story proceeds, Crusoe establishes an increasingly intimate relationship with the reader, confiding in him and inviting him to share his own doubts, mistakes and misfortunes. When struggling to master the art of pottery, for example, Crusoe comments: 'It would make the Reader pity me, or rather laugh at me, to tell how many awkward ways I took to raise this Paste' (p. 120). Or again, when unthinkingly building a boat too far from the sea he acknowledges his own stupidity, saying: 'I went to work upon this Boat, the most like a Fool, that ever Man did, who had any of his Senses awake' (p. 126). This ability to see himself from the outside, to commiserate with himself and recognise his own limitations is one of Crusoe's most endearing features. Gradually the reader builds up a picture of the kind of person Crusoe is: a man who loves order, enjoys solitude, is fond of making neat mental balance sheets of arguments and takes a homely pride in the simple pleasures of domesticity. He frequently criticises himself, as when in the early pages he contrasts his own wilful behaviour with the wise counsel of his father, and observes wryly: 'but other things attended me, and I was still to be the wilful Agent of all my own Miseries'. He is not above laughing at his own foolhardiness, as for example when retrieving articles from the shipwreck he remarks: 'tho' I believe verily, had the calm Weather held, I should have brought away the whole Ship Piece by Piece' (p. 56).

Defoe's style has been described as a 'craving to mimic life itself'.[33] An interesting example of his prose technique which illustrates his skill as a narrator, and incidentally tells us much concerning his hero's character, is the passage describing his various attempts to retrieve articles from the shipwreck. After describing his first successful visit to the wreck and a second visit in which he retrieves two cables and a hawser, he continues:

> But my good Luck began now to leave me; for this Raft was so unweildy, and so overloaden, that after I was enter'd the little Cove, where I had landed the rest of my Goods, not being able to guide it so handily as I did the other, it overset, and threw me and all my Cargoe into the Water; as for my self it was no great Harm, for I was near the Shore; but as to my Cargoe, it was great Part of it lost, especially the Iron, which I expected would have been of great Use to me: However, when the Tide was out, I got most of the Pieces of Cable ashore, and some of the Iron, tho' with infinite Labour; for I was fain to dip for it into the Water, a Work which fatigu'd me very much: After this I went every Day on Board, and brought away what I could get. (p. 56)

The apparent artlessness of the style is deceptive for it contains a number of touches one can easily miss on a first reading. 'But my good Luck began now to leave me' suggests Crusoe is describing an event happening *now* instead of in the past; the words 'began now' gives to the whole paragraph a sense of the present. In describing the sinking of the raft he states simply 'it overset, and threw me and all my Cargoe into the Water'. Again, we notice the active verb *threw*. A phrase such as 'it overset, and all my cargo fell into the water', while conveying a similar meaning, would sound for more prosaic. As it stands, the reader has a vivid sense of Crusoe and all his goods being thoroughly wetted by submersion in the sea. There is also the implied admission that the disaster is his own fault: the raft was 'so overloaden' that he was not able to guide it 'so handily as I did the other'. The remainder of the paragraph is characteristic of Crusoe in that (a) first he tells his reader that the cargo was lost; (b) he then qualifies this by saying that he retrieved most of it; and (c) stresses that all this was only achieved at great pains: 'tho' with infinite Labour', 'a Work which fatigu'd me very much'.

The passage as a whole is typical of many sequences in the novel in that its apparently simple, plodding style conveys much that would otherwise be lost. He describes a series of misfortunes without any trace of self pity – 'as for my self it was no great Harm, for I was near the Shore' – whilst vividly conveying the setback to his plans. The paragraph concludes philosophically: 'After this I went every Day on Board, and brought away what I could get.' Implicit in this sentence is Crusoe's determination not to be defeated by his setback. Despite his misfortune with the overturned raft he is resolved to continue.

One of the enduring fascinations of the narrative is the manner in which Crusoe has to relearn, laboriously and painstakingly, the basic skills necessary for civilised living. In his lifetime Defoe had acquired a fund of knowledge on many different trades and drew on it extensively in his account of his solitary hero mastering the arts of basket-making, pottery, carpentry, baking bread and tailoring. 'I was yet but a very sorry Workman', he acknowledges soon after his arrival on the island, 'tho' Time and Necessity made me a compleat natural Mechanick soon after, as I believe it would do any one else' (p. 72). In saying 'as I believe it would do any one else' Crusoe is being too modest, for what is so remarkable about him is his dogged perseverance in overcoming every obstacle he encounters. He simply refuses to accept defeat. Time and again he reminds his readers of the multitude of tasks involved in the making of bread or the construction of a boat. Many of his readers in 1719 would have been familiar with the skills of bakery and carpentry, but with the passage of time these passages have acquired increasing interest. In an age of specialisation it is salutory to be reminded of the skills of survival. Yet the novel is much more than a parable of economic man. Certainly, an important aspect of it is its insight into *Homo economicus*; its account of the hero's methodical conquest of his environment and the ingenuity with which he learns to survive. But of equal importance is the impact of his experiences on his temperament and attitudes.

Crusoe is by no means a static character. One of the most interesting aspects of the story is the gradual change in his attitude towards the island and his steady growth in wisdom and maturity. His attitude to his predicament, initially one of utter misery, evolves as the story proceeds through dismay, resignation, contentment and affection. At first he refers to the island as 'the Island of Despair' (p. 70) and frequently describes it as 'this horrid Island'. However, when he attempts to circumnavigate it and realises that he may be carried out to sea, his feelings are markedly different: 'Now I look'd back upon my desolate solitary Island, as the most pleasant Place in the World, and all the Happiness my Heart could wish for, was to be there again ... It is scarce possible to imagine the Consternation I was now in, being driven from my beloved Island (for so it appear'd to me now to be) into the wide Ocean' (p. 139). As he becomes reconciled to his solitary life and slowly gains mastery over his domain, he learns to count his blessings and accept his lot with philosophical resignation:

> I gain'd a different Knowledge from what I had before. I entertain'd different Notions of Things. I look'd now upon the World as a Thing remote, which I had nothing to do with, no Expectation from, and indeed no Desires about: In a Word, I had nothing indeed to do with it, nor was ever like to have ... I learn'd to look more upon the bright Side of my Condition, and less upon the dark Side. (pp. 128–30)

This calm, prosaic Crusoe is in total contrast to the raving, despondent castaway who first lands on the shore. He is not only a different person, in the sense that he is reconciled to his fate or no longer pines for civilisation, but he is far more mature in his relationships with others. His wilful disobedience to his father's wishes in the opening pages is a world removed from his solicitude for Friday and his responsible attitude towards those who visit the island. At the outset of his narrative Crusoe confides to his mother that 'my Thoughts were so entirely bent upon seeing the World, that I should never settle to any thing with Resolution enough to go through with it'. As a youth, home and settlement were the very things he had rejected. As a result of his years of solitude he has learned to conquer his restlessness and apply himself with dogged perseverance to a multitude of humdrum tasks. He has domesticated himself and surmounted one obstacle after another with persistence and ingenuity. In this sense a prominent theme of the novel is the exploration of Crusoe's personality. Throughout the story we are privy to his innermost thoughts. We share his inner life and follow the vicissitudes of his conquest of fear and at last the conquest of himself. Through his enforced isolation and the need to recreate civilisation around himself he learns to behave responsibly and in the process becomes a fully adult human being.

One reading of *Robinson Crusoe*, then, is to see it as a novel of discovery on a par with *Gulliver's Travels* or *Great Expectations*, in which a solitary hero learns to triumph over adversity and in the process becomes a wiser and more tolerant being. In this sense the novel belongs to the genre of spiritual autobiography pioneered by Bunyan in *Pilgrim's Progress* and seems to follow logically from the tradition of puritan allegorical writing so popular in the seventeenth and eighteenth centuries.

Crusoe frequently dwells on his isolation. At one point he bemoans the fact that 'I had no Notion of any thing being call'd Deliverance, but my being deliver'd from the Captivity I was in; for tho' I was indeed at large in the Place, yet the Island was certainly a Prison to me' (p. 96). Some years later he reflects again on his predicament and is unsure whether to pity or congratulate himself that 'I seem'd banished from human Society, that I was alone, circumscrib'd by the boundless Ocean, cut off from Mankind, and condemn'd to what I call'd silent Life' (p. 156). The language of confinement – captivity, prison, banished, alone, cut off – is in marked contrast to the language of release with which he begins his story – 'a wandering inclination', 'rambling thoughts', 'an elopement', 'I broke loose'. His ambivalent attitude towards his plight is evident at many points in the story, not least when he confides to the reader that 'I should now tremble at the very Apprehensions of seeing a Man, and was ready to sink into the Ground at but the Shadow or silent Appearance of a Man's having set his Foot in the Island' (p. 156). At one point he even lets slip the phrase 'It was the sixth of November, in the sixth Year of my Reign, or my Captivity, which you please' (p. 137). Reign or captivity: that is the question. On the one hand, Crusoe enjoys 25 years of utter solitude on the island, a period of contentment and resignation. On the other hand, the moment he sees a sail he is consumed with thoughts of release from his loneliness. The island as a symbol of a state of isolation, and Crusoe as a metaphor for the outcast, are never far from the surface of the narrative.

As he becomes reconciled to his fate with the passage of time there is a noticeable shift in his attitude to his solitary condition. At first he bemoans his loneliness, protesting that 'I am singl'd out and separated, as it were, from all the World to be miserable' (p. 66). But after he has lived on the island for two years he 'gave humble and hearty Thanks that God had been pleas'd to discover to me, even that it was possible I might be more happy in this Solitary Condition, than I should have been in a Liberty of Society, and in all the Pleasures of the World' (p. 112). Years later he is confirmed in this view, asking himself 'whether thus conversing mutually with my own Thoughts... was not better than the utmost Enjoyment of humane Society in the World' (p. 136). *Robinson Crusoe* is in one sense a parable on the theme of isolation. During all the years that Crusoe is alone on his island (and for many readers these are by far the most memorable pages of the book) he is fundamentally a happy man, content to follow his familiar routines in a little world of his own making. For all his mishaps and moods of self-doubt, he is in essence at peace with himself. With the coming of human society his real problems begin. He is no longer content to live alone but is tormented with the longing to return to civilisation; he is haunted by fear of the cannibals and of being discovered by intruders. Implicit in Crusoe's dilemma is a wider question: which is the 'real' civilisation – his ordered life on the island, with its simplicity, harmony and contentment; or the world outside, with its greed, violence and selfishness? Crusoe is never basically content once his kingdom has been disturbed by other human beings. It is as if the ending of his solitude marks the termination of his inner happiness.

The arrival of Man Friday on the island and the consequent ending of Crusoe's loneliness is clearly a focal point in the novel's structure (Defoe places the discovery of the footprint in the sand at the exact mid-point of the narrative, as if to emphasise its thematic importance). Crusoe's first sight of the footprint is preceded by the words: 'But now I come to a new Scene of my Life.' It is indeed a watershed, for from this point onwards his life is overshadowed by fear. At first he is convinced the footprint is that of the devil, then realises it must be a savage from the mainland. Friday does not appear until two years after his discovery of the print, years in which Crusoe is beset by fear, doubt and suspicion.

It could be argued that, far from treating Friday as a fellow human being, Crusoe simply domesticates him as if he is another species of animal. Crusoe gives him his name, clothes him, and teaches him the rudiments of English; he insists on being called Master; he teaches Friday the basic skills necessary in a competent and dutiful servant. In all this Friday simply becomes an extension of Crusoe's domain, one more possession to be moulded to his will. As against this one notes the patience with which Crusoe teaches him the elements of conduct and decorum, and imparts to him the skills of survival that he has acquired at such pains. In teaching Friday the arts of husbandry he is repeating the civilising process he has himself undergone and is seeking to mould him into a likeness of himself. Whatever the truth of Crusoe's motives in befriending Friday, the fact remains that the arrival of other human beings marks the end of a long period of contentment. It brings in its train fear and suspicion, and casts a shadow over his island idyll.

Crusoe has originally made much of the fact that the island is a kind of Eden, an enchanted garden untouched by the hand of man. When he fires his rifle for the first time he observes: 'I shot at a great Bird which I saw sitting upon a Tree on the Side of a great Wood, I believe it was the first Gun that had been fir'd there since the Creation of the World' (p. 53). As he widens his knowledge of the island he is increasingly aware of its lush, unspoilt beauty:

> At the End of this March I came to an Opening, where the Country seem'd to descend to the West, and a little Spring of fresh Water which issued out of the Side of the Hill by me, run the other Way, that is due East; and the Country appear'd so fresh, so green, so flourishing, every thing being in a constant Verdure, or Flourish of Spring, that it looked like a planted Garden. I

descended a little on the Side of that delicious Vale, surveying it
with a secret Kind of Pleasure.... (pp. 99–100)

One notes the proliferation of pastoral language: 'country', 'fresh',
'green', 'flourishing', 'verdure', 'garden', 'vale'. When Crusoe first
sets eyes on this land it appears to be untouched by time: it is as if
he is the first human being who has ever set foot on its shores. He is
proud of the fact that he is lord of this domain: 'I was King and
Lord of all this Country indefeasibly, and had a Right of Possession'
(p. 100). His rule brings reason and order to this unspoilt land but
he is horrified to discover that he is not alone, that the island is the
scene of murder and cannibalism by visiting savages. The methodical, painstaking rationality of his own attitude is in blatant contrast
to their bestiality and indifference to human life. The story becomes
a parable of good and evil struggling for the possession of a rural
paradise.

The analogy between the island and the Garden of Eden becomes
more apt when one reflects that Crusoe increasingly takes upon
himself the attributes of a god:

It would have made a Stoic smile to have seen me and my little
Family sit down to Dinner; there was my Majesty the Prince and
Lord of the whole Island; I had the Lives of all my Subjects at my
absolute Command. I could hang, draw, give Liberty, and take it
away, and no Rebels among all my Subjects. (p. 148)

Not only does he regard himself as the supreme ruler of the island
and frequently reflects on this fact, congratulating himself upon it,
but Friday's attitude towards him is one of abject submission. (The
novel can be regarded as a 'god game' romance, a genre in which a
masterful figure on an island assumes the attributes of a divinity. Cf.
Shakespeare's *The Tempest*, R. L. Stevenson's *The Ebb-Tide*, H. G.
Wells's *The Island of Doctor Moreau* and John Fowles's *The Magus*.) In
assuming the role of a god he will not tolerate any opposition to his
rule and expects obedience from all he encounters, whether animal
or human. It is characteristic of him that when an Englishman eventually lands on the island he demands 'That while you stay on this
Island with me, you will not pretend to any Authority here' (p. 256).

His rule, while in a sense despotic, is one of reason and order.
Crusoe is utterly English in his love of tidiness, his liking for
pattern and routine, his methodical approach to all the problems he

encounters. If one views the novel as a parable on the triumph of reason over fear and ignorance, one of the seminal aspects of Crusoe's account is his discovery of a cave which he regards as a haven or retreat:

> I found to my unspeakable Consolation, a meer natural Cave in the Earth, which went in a vast way, and where, I dare say, no Savage, had he been at the Mouth of it, would be so hardy as to venture in, nor indeed, would any Man else; but one who like me, wanted so much as a safe Retreat. (p. 176)

This womb-like cavern proves to be an ideal hiding place from danger – Crusoe describes it as 'a most delightful Cavity', 'a Place of Security', 'such a Retreat as I wanted' – but he is frightened out of his wits by the shining eyes of some unknown creature he disturbs in the entrance. On examination by the light of a flaming torch the creature turns out to be merely an old goat, but Crusoe's initial reaction is one of fear: 'I must confess to you, I made more hast [*sic*] out than I did in, when looking farther into the Place, and which was perfectly dark, I saw two broad shining Eyes of some Creature, whether Devil or Man I knew not' (p. 177). The reference to the devil is interesting and is repeated a few lines later when Crusoe, reasoning with himself, tells himself that 'he that was afraid to see the Devil, was not fit to live twenty Years in an Island all alone'. The unknown thing in the cave proves to have a perfectly natural explanation; Crusoe succeeds in dispelling his fears of the dark and the mysterious by a process of reasoning. The goat is a symbol for the irrational fears which oppress human beings from childhood onwards: once recognised for what it is, it is seen to be harmless. Having conquered his fear of the eyes, Crusoe is then free to explore the rest of the cave which is indeed the haven of his dreams.[34]

To a reader in the late twentieth century, one of the most ambiguous aspects of Crusoe's personality is his constant appeals to a divine power. Again and again he is at pains to express his gratitude for divine intervention, thanking providence for his many blessings. What strikes the reader is that in each case the supposed intervention of providence has a perfectly natural explanation. A notable example of this is when Crusoe shakes out an apparently empty bag of corn and to his astonishment finds ears of barley growing where none had appeared before. At first he believes that 'God had miraculously caus'd this Grain to grow without any Help of Seed sown, and that it was so directed purely for my Sustenance', but on realising that he is mistaken, his faith evaporates: 'and then the Wonder began to cease; and I must confess, my religious Thankfulness to God's Providence began to abate too upon the Discovering that all this was nothing but what was common' (p. 78). A few pages later he repeats his scepticism in even more explicit terms:

> The growing up of the Corn, as is hinted in my Journal, had at first some little Influence upon me, and began to affect me with Seriousness, as long as I thought it had something miraculous in it; but as soon as ever that Part of the Thought was remov'd, all the Impression which was rais'd from it, wore off also, as I have noted already.   (p. 90)

That there is a secular explanation for all he experiences, whether benign or painful, becomes increasingly apparent to him as the story proceeds. The question remains: is Crusoe (and, by implication, Defoe) sincere in his piety, or are the continual references to divine providence meant to be ironic? Are we to infer that Crusoe is deluding himself in his frequent appeals to the supernatural? My own reading tends to support Crusoe's scepticism and would argue that behind his pietistic reflections lies a slowly dawning realisation that reliance on divine power is futile: that Crusoe as an individual and man as a species is alone. Though Crusoe does not say this explicitly it is evident in many of his reflections. Weighing up his predicament, for example, and balancing his fortunes (he is alive and in good health) against his tribulations (he is alone on a remote island subject to earthquakes) he confesses: 'I had no more Sense of God or his Judgments, much less of the present Affliction of my Circumstances being from his Hand, than if I had been in the most prosperous Condition of Life' (p. 90). And again, after his sight of the footprint he confides: 'Thus my Fear banish'd all my religious Hope; all that former Confidence in God which was founded upon such wonderful Experience as I had had of his Goodness, now vanished, as if he that had fed me by Miracle hitherto, could not preserve by his Power the Provision which he had made for me by his Goodness' (p. 156). For its time *Robinson Crusoe* is a remarkably *secular* novel when one reflects that its hero solves every misfortune he encounters through his own efforts, without reliance on divine intervention. Ian Watt has pointed out that, for all Crusoe's pietistic reflections, the actual effect of religion on his behaviour is minimal.[35] In the last analysis he trusts to his own judgement and solves his problems through a calm process of rational thought.

The typical plot of an allegory has been defined as 'one in which the "innocent" – Gulliver, Alice, the Lady in Milton's "Comus", K in Kafka's *The Castle* – is "put through" a series of experiences (tests, traps, fantasy gratifications) which add up to an imaginative analysis of contemporary reality'.[36] Seen in these terms *Robinson Crusoe* can be viewed as an allegory of one man's journey through life. When he lands on the island Crusoe is as naked and helpless as a new-born baby: 'for I was wet, had no Clothes to shift me, nor any thing either to eat or drink to comfort me, neither did I see any Prospect before me, but that of perishing with Hunger, or being devour'd by wild Beasts' (p. 47). As the novel proceeds, his adventures are the story of a gradual conquest of fear and ignorance, a steady extension of knowledge culminating in the triumph of reason. Step by step Crusoe gains control over his environment until at last he has conquered nature and is lord of all he surveys.

On close examination the novel is seen to be structured around a pattern of opposites: order, chaos; savagery, civilisation; domesticity, restlessness; isolation, society; secular, spiritual. The pattern of contrasts is made explicit at many points in the narrative, not least in the fact that Crusoe has two homes – his shelter by the shore and his 'country seat' on the other side of the island. His original dwelling is close to the sea; its proximity to the shore is a reminder to him that 'it was at least possible that something might happen to my Advantage'. His country house is deep inland and he is reluctant to settle there, for 'to enclose my self among the Hills and Woods, in the Center of the Island, was to anticipate my Bondage' (p. 101). The two homes encapsulate Crusoe's divided self and the duality of the novel. His cave by the shore, facing the sea and all it represents, is at once a reminder of his isolation and a promise that one day others may land there and rescue him from his plight. It is a tangible link with the shipwreck and the world of men. His country seat, surrounded by greenery and cut off from the sea, stands for all that is insular and reclusive in his temperament. Enclosed and hidden, it is the confirmation of his loneliness. The two thus embody the competing tensions in his makeup: whether to look outward to the sea in the hope of release, or inward to the island in resignation to his fate. Restlessness or contentment, sociability or isolation – these are the dilemmas of Crusoe's life.

Ian Watt has demonstrated convincingly that 'Robinson Crusoe is certainly the first novel in the sense that it is the first fictional narrative in which an ordinary person's daily activities are the centre of continuous literary attention'.[37] The continuing fascination of the book lies not only in the fact that the reader shares with its central character the multitude of small events which make up a human life, but in the nature of Crusoe himself. It is such an intensely *personal* book and written with such conviction that one senses Defoe's emotional involvement on almost every page. In the Preface to *David Copperfield*, another *Bildungsroman* written 130 years later, Dickens wrote: 'no one can ever believe this Narrative, in the reading, more than I believed it in the writing'. The same is surely true of *Robinson Crusoe*. In scene after scene of the narrative – the landing on the island, the retrieval of goods from the wreck, the construction of the shelter, the voyage round the island, the making of pottery, the discovery of the footprint – one senses an intensely visual authorial presence. Defoe is, as it were, looking over Crusoe's shoulder, living his experiences with him and sharing the plethora of mundane tasks which constitute his daily life. It is not simply that Crusoe himself engages our sympathy and understanding as we follow his fluctuating moods but that all he experiences can be touched and felt. There is a powerful sense of reality; this, one feels, actually happened. Unlike the 'I' of many first-person narratives, Crusoe becomes a character in his own right, a fully realised human being with strengths and weaknesses in abundance. It is for these reasons that *Crusoe* can surely claim to be a novel. If one accepts Watt's definition that a novel is 'a full and authentic report of human experience'[38] then Defoe's first full-length work of fiction is supremely that: an impressively truthful chronicle of all that one man experienced and felt.

Yet were *Robinson Crusoe* only that, one doubts if it would have come to occupy such a central place in literary history. Its lasting significance surely lies in its consummate blending of divergent literary traditions and its fruitfulness as a source of myth. The Defoe scholar Pat Rogers has pointed out that *Robinson Crusoe* 'exhibits, along with sustained mastery of narrative, a capacity to dramatise spiritual and psychological experience which opened up fictional possibilities which have still not been exhausted'.[39] In achieving this the novel represents a fusion of two literary traditions: the adventure romance and the allegory of moral discovery. The romance, as exemplified by *Don Quixote* (1605) and *Gil Blas* (1715), is a narrative characterised by exotic adventure rather than realistic incident. The romance is typified by vivid scenes and picaresque exploits with comparatively little attention to the development of character. The moral allegory, as exemplified by *The Pilgrim's Progress* (1678) depicts a journey through a symbolic landscape in which the central figure moves from innocence to enlightenment. *Robinson Crusoe* fuses the two genres in a coherent narrative which is both a detailed chronicle of one man's life and an allegory which is of continuing relevance to modern man.

For the central dilemma posed by the novel – can man survive in isolation, or is he wholly dependent on the society of others? – remains as pertinent today as ever. In exploring this dilemma through the story of a lone survivor cast away on a desert island, Defoe created a novel of discovery which hauntingly illuminates the nature of man. The basic situation of an individual cut off from his fellow men and having to rely on his own ingenuity in order to survive has proved to be a most fruitful myth. But *Crusoe* is not simply a 'survival' novel *par excellence* but a novel of exploration rich in insights into human nature. Not only does Crusoe explore his island from end to end but he explores *himself*, with total honesty. In doing so he sees himself without illusions, reveals man at his noblest and basest, and anticipates the work of Conrad, Wells and Golding.

Memoirs of a Cavalier

Most critical studies of Defoe's fiction pass over *Memoirs of a Cavalier* without comment. It tends to share the fate of *The Further Adventures of Robinson Crusoe* and *A New Voyage Round the World* and to be dismissed as a lesser work hardly worthy of inclusion in the canon. Though it undoubtedly has many defects – it bears all the hallmarks of being hastily written, it suffers from repetitiveness, and cannot be said to have a plot – it would be unfair to dismiss it out of hand. It is by no means devoid of literary interest and its recent reappearance in print after being unobtainable for many years suggests that the tide of critical opinion may be turning in its favour.

The opening pages create the impression that one is about to read a *Bildungsroman* in the vein of *David Copperfield*. There are detailed particulars of the date and place of the narrator's birth, a hint of unusual events to follow – 'the consequences of my life may allow me to suppose some extraordinary influence affected my birth', an account of his parentage and early life. But the remainder of the book fails to fulfil the promise of its opening sequence, for *Memoirs of a Cavalier* is in no sense a *Bildungsroman*. The Cavalier himself, unlike Robinson Crusoe or Roxana, is a static character: he reacts to events but does not change or develop his own personality. In this respect the story lacks the psychological depth of *Crusoe* or *Moll Flanders*. It succeeds admirably as a work of reportage but is not a novel of character in the same sense as they are.

On the other hand, he is rather more than a cipher. For example, he is not afraid to tell stories against himself, as when he recounts the episode of his attempted seduction by a courtesan (pp. 32–4). This incident, which presents him in a rather unfavourable light by exposing his naïveté, is told with all Defoe's customary realism. When the courtesan makes advances towards him he has to admit that 'I was all over disorder and distraction', and confesses that after their parting he has a strong inclination to visit her again. The Cavalier, though lacking in solidity as a character, is a fallible human being who is not afraid to admit his own weaknesses.

The events depicted in the *Memoirs* take place during the years 1631–48 and purport to be the recollections of a soldier who took part in the Thirty Years War in Germany and in the English Civil War. Part One, describing his experiences in the army of the King of Sweden (a champion of protestantism) covers the years 1631–41, and Part Two, describing his adventures as a soldier in the Royal Army of King Charles I, covers the period 1642–8. Since the entire narrative is cast in the first person and gives an eye-witness account of numerous battles and campaigns, the book as a whole gives a powerful sense of history in the making. Clearly, Defoe intended to give an impression of war reported at first hand from the standpoint of an ordinary foot soldier, and to a large measure succeeds in this intention.

He culled his information from a variety of written sources, including Clarendon's *History of the Rebellion*, the *Swedish Intelligencer* and Bulstrode Whitelocke's *Memorials of the English Affairs*, reconstructing his data to create the illusion of a personal account. The fact that the Cavalier claims to be an eye-witness of the battles he is describing lends an air of authenticity to the narrative that it would otherwise lack. Typical of his approach is his account of the battle of the river Lech, one of the decisive campaigns of the Thirty Years War:

> I shall be the longer in relating this account of the Lech, being esteemed in those days as great an action as any battle or siege of that age, and particularly famous for the disaster of the gallant old General Tilly; and for that I can be more particular in it than other accounts, having been an eye-witness to every part of it.
>
> (p. 87)

Similar phrases recur throughout the narrative: 'I am the more particular in this Relation, having been an Eye-Witness of the Action' (p. 242); 'it is not my Design to write a History of any more of these Wars than I was actually concerned in' (p. 110); 'the History of the Times will supply the Particulars which I omit, being willing to confine my self to my own Accounts and Observations' (p. 270). The weakness of the first-person method is that Defoe has constantly to fashion his materials in such a way as to make it plausible for his narrator to be an eye-witness of every skirmish and encounter he describes: if there is a battle he did not participate in, he cannot describe it – as in the closing engagements of the Civil War, where he admits lamely: 'I was quite disconsolate at the News of this last Action, and the more because I was not there' (p. 257).

Conversely, the first-person narration gives a strong sense of immediacy to the events described. The account, one feels, is reliable because the cavalier was *there*. He is describing what he saw and knew.

Defoe was a highly skilled fabricator, and as a journalist, pamphleteer and editor of *The Review* he had acquired considerable expertise in the invention of seemingly authentic narratives. Not only was he a past master in the art of counterfeiting apparently realistic autobiographical accounts, but he possessed an almost uncanny ability to reach inside the characters he had created: to *become* them. *Memoirs of a Cavalier*, for all its imperfections, creates the illusion of factuality. Though the reader is inwardly aware this *is* an illusion, it is all too easy to accept the book at face value as a contemporary eye-witness account written by a soldier. On taking part in the Civil War, for example, the narrator vividly conveys what it must have felt like to slaughter one's fellow countrymen in the heat of battle:

> I was now, by the King's particular Favour, summoned to the Councils of War, my Father continuing absent and ill; and now I began to think of the real Grounds, and which was more, of the fatal Issue of this War. I say, I now began it; for I cannot say that I ever rightly stated Matters in my own Mind before, though I had been enough used to Blood, and to see the Destruction of People, sacking of Towns, and plundering the Country; yet 'twas in Germany, and among Strangers; but I found a strange secret and unaccountable Sadness upon my Spirits to see this acting in my own native Country. It grieved me to the Heart, even in the Rout of our Enemies, to see the Slaughter of them; and even in the Fight, to hear a Man cry for Quarter in English, moved me to a Compassion which I had never been used to; nay, sometimes it looked to me as if some of my own Men had been beaten; and when I heard a Soldier cry, O God, I am shot, I looked behind me to see which of my own Troop was fallen. Here I saw my self at the cutting of the Throats of my Friends; and indeed some of my near Relations.   (pp. 164–5)

The Cavalier's 'strange secret and unaccountable Sadness' heightens the impression of a nation at war with itself. In describing the slaughter and confusion inseparable from civil war the narrative anticipates the global perspective of such 'disaster' novels as

Wells's *The War of the Worlds* and Camus's *The Plague*. There is the same sense of detachment, an awareness that the narrator is both a personal witness (and therefore emotionally involved) and a chronicler determined to present a factual account (and therefore obliged to conceal nothing from the reader). The phrase 'to hear a Man cry for Quarter... moved me to a Compassion which I had never been used to' is wrung from him in spite of himself. Here is a professional soldier, a man hardened to battle, freely admitting to compassion for those he has wounded.

The book is a novel of action which anticipates the pace and adventure of Stevenson's *Kidnapped*. Defoe enlivens his rather dry account of military campaigns with vivid incidents which remain in the imagination through their extraordinary realism. A particularly interesting example of this is the discovery of a purse concealed inside a horse's saddle:

> As I was riding between Leipsick and Hall I observed my Horse went very aukwardly and uneasy, and sweat very much, though the Weather was cold, and we had rid but very softly; I fancied therefore that the Saddle might hurt the Horse, and calls my new Captain up; George say I, I believe this Saddle hurts the Horse; so we alighted and looking under the Saddle found the Back of the Horse extreamly galled; so I bid him take off the Saddle, which he did, and giving the Horse to my young Leipsicker to lead, we sat down to see if we could mend it, for there was no Town near us; Says George, pointing with his Finger, if you please to cut open the Pannel there, I'll get something to stuff into it which will bear if from the Horse's Back; so while he look'd for something to thrust in, I cut a Hole in the Pannel of the Saddle, and following it with my Finger I felt something hard, which seemed to move up and down; again as I thrust it with my Finger, here's something that should not be here, says I, not yet imagining what afterwards fell out, and calling, run back, bad him put up his Finger; whatever 'tis, says he, 'tis this hurts the horse, for it bears just on his Back when the Saddle is set on; so we strove to take hold on it, but could not reach it; at last we took the upper Part of the Saddle quite from the Pannel, and there lay a small Silk Purse wrapt in a Piece of Leather, and full of Gold Ducats.   (p. 69)

If there was any uncertainty concerning the authorship of *Memoirs of a Cavalier* this passage would surely remove any doubts, for it contains unmistakable evidence of Defoe's style.[40] One notes the rather ponderous conversational manner: the entire paragraph is one long sentence broken up by semicolons. One notes also the accumulation of corroborative detail: we learn where the incident took place, what the weather was like, what the narrator and his companion said to one another, what the purse was made of. Characteristically, we are given additional information – the horse had been ridden 'but very softly', 'there was no Town near us', the purse was wrapped in a piece of leather. The change of tense from past to present creates the illusion that the events occur at the moment of narration: 'Says George, pointing with his Finger'; 'here's something that should not be here, says I'; 'whatever 'tis, says he, 'tis this hurts the Horse, for it bears just on his Back'. Notice also the precision of the description – it is so detailed that it might be a film set. Defoe is not content simply to state that the two alighted from their horses, he tells us that they sat down by the roadside, that his companion pointed with his finger, that the Cavalier called to him and, running back, urges him to place his finger in the cavity, that the purse could not be reached at the first attempt. The passage as a whole is an instance of his ability to conjure up a memorable scene from the most commonplace materials. It is not consciously 'literary' or artistic, yet it is fixed indelibly in the mind because of its authenticity. The narrator observes that his horse is sweating despite the fact that the day is cold: from this simple observation stems a scene which is realistic in every particular.

In writing the supposed *Memoirs* Defoe adopted a number of literary devices which have since become commonplace in works of this kind. The text is introduced by a Preface alleging that the manuscript was discovered by accident many years previously among the private papers of an eminent government minister. The Preface quotes a memorandum, signed with the initials 'L. K.', stating: 'I found this Manuscript among my father's writings.' The elaborate attempt to demonstrate the genuineness of the account is characteristic of Defoe's first-person narratives, as is the insistence on the author's anonymity: 'It may suffice the reader, without being very inquisitive after my name, that I was born in the County of Salop, in the year 1608.' These conventions – an insistence that the manuscript is contemporary with the events depicted; the assertion of its discovery among valuable papers; and the attempt to protect the identity of the writer – are designed to establish the provenance of the text by giving it a spurious air of legitimacy. In common with Walpole's *The Castle of Otranto* and Wells's *The Island of Doctor Moreau,* the author is keen to create the appearance of authenticity. This is achieved through a series of pretences designed to mask the fictiveness of the text and above all by a documentary, matter-of-fact tone of narration ideally suited to its purpose.

James Sutherland has described Defoe's forte as the 'imaginative manipulation of printed sources'.[41] Next to *A Journal of the Plague Year, Memoirs of a Cavalier* is the supreme example of his ability to digest a mass of published material and refashion it from an auto-biographical perspective. To read it is to enter imaginatively into the life and times of a professional soldier in the seventeenth century and to marvel at Defoe's power to bring facts so vigorously to life.

Captain Singleton

If *Robinson Crusoe* is the story of one man's journey from civilisation to solitude, *Captain Singleton* is the reverse: the account of one man's voyage from isolation to dependence. The central metaphor of the novel is that of navigation: life as a journey. Throughout the story there is a continual obsession with direction, with points of the compass. Whether on land or sea Singleton is preoccupied with the questions: Where are we? Which way are we heading? What is our destination? His narrative is not only a physical journey, in the sense that the novel is an exciting adventure story in Africa and on the high seas, but an emotional journey (from loneliness towards dependence) and a mental journey (from innocence towards wisdom). It is also a symbolic journey dramatising the human adventure with all its vicissitudes of happiness, fear and pain. On each of these levels *Captain Singleton* merits careful study as an experiment in narrative form and a prototype of the odyssey novels of Melville and Conrad.

The first half of the book, describing the epic journey by Singleton and his companions across the mainland of Africa, is a vividly written account penned long before the explorations of Mungo Park and Stanley. Africa in 1720 was still an unknown quantity (as late as 1860 maps showed the interior of the continent as a vast empty space) and the landscape depicted by Defoe is almost wholly imaginary. It was not until 1875 that Stanley traced the route of the Congo to the Atlantic; at the time Defoe was writing he had to rely on the conjectures of eighteenth-century mapmakers supplemented by his own powers of invention. Singleton describes the decision to cross Africa from Mozambique to Angola – a journey of some 1500 miles from east to west – as 'one of the rashest and wildest, and most desperate Resolutions that ever was taken by Man, or any Number of Men, in the World' (p. 47). His account of his adventures across rivers, lakes, deserts and forests forms an extraordinarily sustained piece of storytelling in which the author relies on the intense contemporary interest in exploration. The promise on the title page that the book contains 'an Account of the Customs and Manners of the People' together with a description of 'His great Deliverances from the barbarous Natives and wild Beasts' is amply fulfilled. Defoe allows his imagination free rein in visualising encounters with strange animals, cannibals, natural obstacles and a wild and inhospitable terrain. Continually the travellers are battling against a hostile or indifferent universe as they surmount one hindrance after another, overcoming each difficulty in their path through their own resourcefulness. Through all his account of adventure and exploration Singleton is at pains to reduce his experiences to a human scale by the introduction of homely detail. Thus, a river is described as 'not above as broad as the Thames is at Windsor'; at another stage it is so shallow 'there was not water enough to swim a London wherry'; a herd of wild creatures are standing 'as thick as a Drove of Bullocks going to a Fair'; a cloud of sand reminds him of 'the Roads in Summer, when it is very dusty, and a large Drove of Cattle are coming, only very much greater'.⁴² Through such analogies he enables the reader to relate the alien world of Africa to the known and familiar.

Defoe was extremely interested in pirates and his vivid account of Singleton's exploits as the leader of a crew of buccaneers owes much to his own work *The King of Pirates* (1719) and anticipates his much fuller *A General History of the Pirates* (1724). With considerable gusto Singleton describes encounter after encounter in which he and his men seize ships and goods and accumulate vast stores of wealth and possessions. At last the reiteration of one raid after another becomes wearisome and one senses his relief when, tiring of the continual catalogue of destruction and theft, he remarks: 'I resolved now that we would leave off being Pirates, and turn Merchants' (p. 199). What interests Defoe is not so much piracy in itself but its corrupting influences on human nature in general and on Singleton in particular. At first Singleton seems to feel little compunction for the recital of crime he describes. He is apparently amoral, caring little for law or morality. But niggles of conscience begin to trouble him until at last a violent thunderstorm seems to embody his worst premonitions of divine judgment:

> As for my self, I must confess my Eyes were open to my Danger, tho' not the least to any thing of Application for Remedy. I was all Amazement and Confusion, and this was the first Time that I can say I began to feel the Effects of that Horror which I know since much more of, upon the just Reflection on my former Life. I thought my self doom'd by Heaven to sink that Moment into eternal Destruction; and with this peculiar Mark of Terror, viz. That the Vengeance was not executed in the ordinary Way of

human Justice, but that God had taken me into his immediate Disposing, and had resolved to be the Executor of his own Vengeance. (p. 195)

This is a powerfully written passage in which one is aware of Singleton expressing remorse for his past behaviour – 'upon the just Reflection on my former Life' – and Defoe censuring his own creation for his errant ways – 'That the Vengeance was not executed in the ordinary Way of human Justice'. His disquiet on experiencing 'the Effects of that Horror which I know since much more of' is an indication of his divided nature and strikingly anticipates the inner torment of Stevenson's narrators. [43]

Through all his adventures on land and sea one is aware of a gradual shift in his responses to society. The novel is a *Bildungsroman* in the sense that the narrator tells the story of his journey through life from childhood to maturity, and in the process reveals much of his own attitude to human society. One of the dominant motifs of the novel is the human need for dependence. Reflecting on his experiences and on all that life has taught him Singleton concludes: 'for really a Man that has no Subsistence, and no Residence, no Place that has a Magnetick influence upon his Affections, is in one of the most odd uneasy Conditions in the World'. (p. 276). At the outset of his adventures he is without dependants, a man utterly alone. He is a waif who knows almost nothing about his origins. On returning to England after his African adventures he bemoans the fact that 'I had neither Friend, Relation, nor Acquaintance in England, tho' it was my Native Country' (p. 137). During the second half of the novel describing his piratical adventures he becomes more and more dependent on William Walters, the Quaker, who becomes an increasingly important source of advice, counsel and influence. His reliance on William is such that by the end of the story William has become a surrogate father, providing him with the reassurance and stability he would otherwise have lacked. Singleton comes to accept the truth that his life began in a state of utter alienation from society and has culminated in reliance on a fellow human being. 'William was a wise and wary Man', he concludes, 'and indeed all the Prudentials of my Conduct had for a long Time been owing to his Advice' (p. 265)

In this sense the novel can be seen as the story of a quest for anchorage, a search for the fulfilment which can only be found in human society. When in the course of his African adventures

Singleton encounters a lone Englishman, he is deeply impressed by the man's predicament and by the fact that 'when he could get away from us for a little, we saw him walking alone, and shewing all the most extravagent Tokens of an ungovernable Joy' (p. 121). The Englishman is so relieved to see them that he exclaims 'to be sure wherever we were a-going, we came from Heaven, and were sent on purpose to save him from the most wretched Condition that ever Man was reduced to' (p. 122). Singleton describes the white man's plight as 'his very unhappy Circumstance', 'his miserable Circumstance', 'the most wretched Condition'. Clearly, for him solitude is a plight to be avoided at all costs. He feels deeply for the Englishman's loneliness and shares his joy at his rescue. The episode echoes Crusoe's rescue from his lonely island, but whereas *Robinson Crusoe* is described from the inside, the encounter in *Captain Singleton* is described from the outside looking in. It is as if Crusoe is being observed from another vantage point: he is the lonely castaway seen from the perspective of his deliverers. The shift in point of view enables the reader to share with the recluse his happiness on being reunited with his kindred and to possess a deeper understanding of Singleton's own predicament.

On his own admission Singleton embarks on his adventures in a state of naïveté: 'I was now to enter upon a Part of independent Life, a thing I was indeed very ill prepared to manage; for I was perfectly loose and dissolute in my Behaviour, bold and wicked while I was under Government, and now perfectly unfit to be trusted with Liberty' (p. 11). As the story proceeds a change in Singleton's attitudes becomes evident. Through the buffetings of experience he slowly learns to have more concern for his fellows and to accept responsibility for the men who look to him for leadership. Slowly his indifference to others is modified by a recognition of their reliance upon him, a process which begins long before his meeting with William Walters (though it is greatly accelerated by the Quaker's example). At the commencement of his African journey, for example, he confides to the reader: 'Before I go any farther, I must hint to the Reader, that from this time forward I began to enter a little more seriously into the Circumstance I was in, and concern'd my self more in the Conduct of our Affairs' (p. 54). He begins to recognise that he possesses qualities of leadership and decision that are valued by those under him and to accept that he is responsible for their well-being. As his friendship with William deepens he gradually absorbs the Quaker's moral values and respect for human life until at last he is struck by remorse for all he has done. He reflects bitterly that 'the Work that remain'd was gentler than the Labour past, *viz. Repentance*, and that it was high Time to think of it; I say these, and such Thoughts as these engross'd my Hours, and in a Word, I grew very sad' (p. 265). His acceptance of his responsibility for his own actions and that he is accountable to his conscience for his apparent indifference to human suffering forms one of the important subsidiary themes of the narrative. From being a man with no scruples he emerges as a true friend, a chastened figure who experiences strong emotions of sadness, compassion and loyalty. His surname aptly suggests his independent nature; the novel is in a real sense the account of one man's journey from isolation to community, from innocence to maturity.

In common with Stevenson's *An Inland Voyage* and Conrad's *Heart of Darkness*, the novel is at once an exciting tale of travel and adventure and a metaphorical representation of the human journey. The duality between factual history and parable gives an ambivalence to the narrative which is particularly evident in the image of the desert that has to be crossed:

> Having with infinite labour mounted these Hills, and coming to a View of the Country beyond them, it was indeed enough to astonish as stout a Heart as ever was created. It was a vast howling Wilderness, not a Tree, a River, or a Green thing to be seen, for as far as the Eye could look; nothing but a scalding Sand, which, as the Wind blew, drove about in Clouds, enough to overwhelm Man and Beast; nor could we see any End of it, either before us, which was our Way, or to the right Hand or left: So that truly our Men began to be discouraged, and talk of going back again; nor could we indeed think of venturing over such a horrid Place as that before us, in which we saw nothing but present Death. (p. 179)

The travellers are faced with the choice of continuing with their journey, with all the unknown dangers this involves, or turning back and conceding defeat. Their decision to cross the wilderness is one of the turning points of the novel and a triumph of the human spirit. Undoubtedly Defoe intended his readers to draw an analogy between this inhospitable wilderness and the human journey from innocence to experience. In his own lifetime he had surmounted setback after setback, undergoing imprisonment, bankruptcy, ridicule and ostracism in his quest for fulfilment. Singleton is an archetypal Defoe hero in his dogged pursuit of his goals and his resolve not to be deflected by faint-heartedness or caution. His journey across the trackless wastes not only echoes the wanderings of the Israelites from Egypt to the promised land, but symbolises the journey of the human spirit – not simply the outward journey from innocence to enlightenment but the spiritual voyage towards the innermost regions of the mind. Defoe was well aware of the dark recesses of anger, violence and fear that lie beneath the veneer of rationality – Crusoe's moods of despair and self-doubt bear abundant witness to his awareness of man's frailty – and it is not difficult to see in Singleton's crossing of the wasteland a metaphor for man's coming to terms with his own nature. For Singleton, as for Defoe, man has no choice but to cross the desert: 'And therefore, upon the whole, he proposed that we should attempt this Desert, and perhaps we should not find it so long as we feared' (p. 80).

He accepts that there can be no shirking of the challenge, that there are situations in life when one has no alternative but to cross the divide, however unpalatable. In facing this truth he makes one of the key decisions of his maturity and transforms the novel from a simple adventure story to a spiritual odyssey of continuing relevance to our times. Singleton's heart of darkness – his 'vast howling Wilderness' – is the unknown region that lies at the heart of man and haunts the novels of Wells and Golding. Looking back on Defoe's story from a late twentieth-century perspective we can recognise it as a precursor of their work and one of the earliest explorations of the Africas of the mind.

James Sutherland has remarked of *Captain Singleton* that 'the interest of the book depends largely on what happens next; on dangerous situations, difficulties overcome, escapes, surprises, and discoveries'.[44] It is in fact a classic instance of the adventure narrative exemplified by such tales as Stevenson's *St Ives* or Poe's *The Narrative of Arthur Gordon Pym* – a story in which a first-person narrator embarks on a long journey or series of exploits and recounts his experiences and all he undergoes in the course of his wanderings. The limitation of the genre is that it is difficult to sustain the reader's interest without introducing diversions and incidents which almost inevitably seem contrived. In fairness to Defoe it has to be said that he succeeds remarkably well in weaving together a coherent and readable story, but there are moments when interest begins to flag and the continual need to invent becomes apparent.

One of the weaknesses which can legitimately be attributed to the novel lies in the character of Singleton himself. For it is arguable that as a central figure he is not drawn in any depth, that he lacks psychological substance. He is simply the narrator, responding to events as they occur but contributing little of his own volition to the exciting story he unfolds. Placed alongside William he seems a comparatively passive figure. Indeed, it is arguable that as a character William is drawn with so much more subtlety that he dominates the second half of the novel; that in comparison with him Singleton increasingly recedes. Whereas Singleton lacks a distinctive authorial voice, the reader is drawn more and more to William's sagacity and dry sense of humour.

Towards the end of his narrative Singleton reflects on his loneliness, bemoaning the fact that he is destitute of a friend. He considers the idea of proposing marriage to William's sister: 'and having resolved to make her the Object of my first Bounty, I did not doubt but I should purchase something of a Refuge for my self, and a kind of a Centre, to which I should tend my future Actions' (p. 276). His acknowledgement that he is without a centre is revealing, for he not only lacks a fixed point of reference, in the sense that his restlessness makes it difficult for him to remain for long in one place, but seems to lack solidarity by comparison with Crusoe or Moll Flanders. Such a reading of the novel fails to take account of the care with which Defoe develops Singleton's character – in particular his gradual assumption of leadership and the slow but unmistakable change in his attitudes towards remorse. Though not drawn with the same skill or depth as Crusoe, in common with Crusoe he is not a static figure but a character who gradually changes his attitudes and behaviour in response to events. The real strength of the novel lies in the relationship between Singleton and William Walters. It seems clear that William's increasing domination of the narrative is an intentional device and that Defoe wanted William's qualities of resourcefulness, wisdom and caution to be seen as a contrast to the narrator's impulsiveness and amorality.

From the standpoint of literary history, and in particular Defoe's contribution to the development of the novel, one of the most significant aspects of the narrative is Defoe's growing mastery of dialogue. The conversations between Singleton and William, initially stilted and artificial, become increasingly animated until one is caught unawares by this kind of exchange:

Say any Thing to me, William, said I, I will take it kindly: I began now to be very much moved at his Discourse.

Says William, Tears running down his Face, it is because Men live as if they were never to dye, that so many dye before they know how to live; but it was not Death that I meant, when I said, That there was something to be thought of beyond this Way of Living.

Why, William, said I, what was that?

It was Repentance, says he.

Why, says I, did you ever know a Pirate repent?

At this he started a little, and return'd, at the Gallows, I have one before, and I hope thou wilt be the second.

He spoke this very affectionately, and with an Appearance of Concern for me.

Well, William, says I, I thank you, and I am not so senseless of these Things, perhaps, as I make my self seem to be; but come, let me hear your Proposal.

My Proposal, says William, is for thy Good, as well as my own; we may put an End to this kind of Life, and repent; and I think the fairest Occasion offers for both at this very Time that ever did, or ever will, or indeed, can happen again.

Look you, William, says I, let me have your Proposal for putting an End to our present Way of Living first, for that is the Case before us, and you and I will talk of the other afterward. I am not so insensible, said I, as you may think me to be; but let us get out of this hellish Condition we are in first.

Nay, says William, thou art in the right there; we must never talk of repenting while we continue Pirates.   (pp. 258–9)

With the minimum of words Defoe powerfully suggests the emotional force of the conversation ('I began now to be very much moved', 'He spoke this very affectionately') whilst at the same time hinting at the shift in Singleton's attitudes wrought by his friend's arguments. William's declaration, 'It is because Men live as if they were never to dye, that so many dye before they know how to live', has undeniable eloquence; the reader senses that for him this confrontation is of crucial significance in turning Singleton's thoughts towards repentance. Throughout the exchange one senses the Quaker's genuine concern for his protagonist and his anxiety to convince the other of the error of his ways. Simultaneously we are aware of Singleton's reluctant admission of the force of William's arguments. William is both supplicant and counsellor, conscious of his subordinate position yet at the same time determined to bring home to the Captain the folly of his actions. He does not mince words in the debate but speaks his mind outright – 'we may put an End to this kind of Life, and repent' – aware that in doing so he risks incurring the Captain's anger and may forfeit his trust. Singleton's growing respect for William's sagacity and the slow emergence of their mutual affection for one another forms a powerful undercurrent in the novel, and one which merits close attention.

In writing the story of Captain Singleton and his adventures as explorer and pirate, Defoe was clearly feeling his way towards the full-scale novel of human relationships as exemplified by *Moll Flanders*. By comparison with this the earlier narrative seems an apprentice effort, an uneasy hybrid between novel and romance. But despite its limitations *Captain Singleton* is a marked advance on the adventure narrative exemplified by *The King of Pirates* and *Memoirs of a Cavalier*. In its extensive use of dialogue, its use of humour and anecdote, its neat transition between the two halves of the narrative, and its blending of the actual and the symbolic the novel represents a bridge between the desert island romance of *Robinson Crusoe* and the urban panorama of *Moll Flanders*. The book is in a real sense the workshop in which Defoe finally mastered the narrative form and grasped the full possibilities of the autobiographical novel.

Moll Flanders

What manner of work is *Moll Flanders*? In his preface Defoe, with his customary disingenuousness, asserts that it is not a work of fiction but a 'private History':

> The World is so taken up of late with Novels and Romances, that it will be hard for a private History to be taken for Genuine, where the Names and other Circumstances of the Person are concealed, and on this Account we must be content to leave the Reader to pass his own Opinion upon the ensuing Sheets, and take it just as he pleases.

This is of course written tongue in cheek, but its language is worth attention as a statement of authorial intention. The book was published in 1722, when the novel as a literary genre was still a very new fledgling. The statement that 'the World is so taken up of late with Novels and Romances' can only refer to his own *Robinson Crusoe* and *Captain Singleton*, both of which are fictional narratives masquerading as true autobiographical accounts. Clearly, Defoe wishes his readers to accept *Moll Flanders* as genuine, whilst acknowledging that he must be content 'to leave the Reader to pass his own Opinion...and take it just as he pleases'. In fact he goes to great lengths to give the work an internal consistency and the hallmarks of an autobiographical confession. In its geographical and chronological detail, its time scheme, its references to actual people and places and its overall air of veracity the novel is one of Defoe's most convincing and satisfying productions.[45]

Though *Robinson Crusoe* and *Moll Flanders* are the work of the same author they seem on first consideration to be totally different entities. Where *Crusoe* is relatively static and solitary, *Moll* is fluid and social; where *Crusoe* has as its focal point life on a desert island, *Moll* ranges widely over London and England. On closer examination it can be seen that the two novels have in common a preoccupation with human psychology. The thesis of each story is a quest for survival, a search for economic and social stability. The central character in each case is striving to achieve independence and self-sufficiency in the face of adversity; both novels are object lessons in

95

perseverance. Robinson Crusoe and Moll Flanders both succeed in engaging our sympathy and understanding largely because we identify with them in their struggle to bring life under control and master their own destinies. What generations of readers have admired in them both is their sheer determination to survive.

One of the many reasons why *Moll Flanders* is such a fascinating novel is its dual perspective. The story is ostensibly narrated by a 70-year-old woman, a reformed criminal, looking back on her past life and commenting on her youthful self from the vantage point of maturity and repentance. Thus, the narrator is simultaneously the wayward girl who moves at breathtaking pace through a sequence of picaresque adventures and the mature woman unfolding her story to the reader with mingled understanding and regret. This alone would be sufficient to account for the novel's duality, but behind this fact lies a deeper ambivalence. When reading *Moll* we are faced with two questions: What is the narrator's attitude to her own life? And what is the reader's attitude towards her? Behind these questions lies a third: What is Defoe's attitude towards his own creation?

Though Defoe was a master of the autobiographical form, its limitation is that the reader sees the narrator from only one point of view: there is no perspective except Moll's own. (The only exception to this is the Preface, where there is an attempt to summarise her life and behaviour from the standpoint of a judicious observer.) The consequence is that Moll is her own accuser. She evaluates her actions and passes judgement on her own moral lapses, but we do not see her from the outside. Had Defoe chosen to tell her story in the third person it would be interesting to see her from a different perspective, for example, that of her first lover or one of her husbands. As it is, she is both judge and jury, the central figure in a long and diverse narrative seen from a single focus.

In his novel *Tono-Bungay* H. G. Wells wrote: 'It is wonderful what people the English are for keeping up pretences.'[46] This might almost be taken as the theme of *Moll Flanders*, for in a sense the entire story is one of pretence and disguise. At the outset we learn that her name is fictitious:

My True Name is so well known in the records, or Registers at Newgate, and in the Old Bailey, and there are some things of such Consequence still depending there, relating to my particular Conduct, that it is not to be expected I should set my Name, or the Account of My Family to this Work.   (p. 7)

The story of her life from her lowly beginnings onward is one of concealment – not simply of her true identity but of her poverty, her status and her nature. Time and again when evading pursuers or seeking anonymity she adopts a disguise, either by changing her clothes or passing herself off as a widow. Typical of this process is her decision, following her second unfortunate marriage, to become in effect a different person: 'I resolved therefore, as to the State of my present Circumstances; that it was absolutely Necessary to change my Station, and make a new Appearance in some other Place where I was not known, and even to pass by another Name if I found Occasion' (p. 76). The assumption of one persona after another becomes a way of life for her, culminating in the moment of revelation in Newgate prison when she is overcome with remorse for her past deeds: 'in a word, I was perfectly changed, and became another Body' (p. 281).

Moll's chameleon-like ability to assume a different identity almost at will is more than a question of changing her clothes or adopting a pseudonym. It could be argued that her whole life is one long pretence, and that through much of her narrative she is guilty of self-delusion. This raises the question: which is the 'real' Moll Flanders? Is it the elderly, penitent Moll who is telling the story, or the wily, unscrupulous woman who dominates much of the action? The fact that she is simultaneously both sinner and penitent means that is is difficult to arrive at a conclusive answer.

Moll herself tells us that her decision to tell the story of her life in such detail has a didactic intention: 'As the publishing this Account of my Life, is for the sake of the just Moral of every part of it, and for Instruction, Caution, Warning and Improvement to every Reader' (p. 326). Her life story can be seen as a kind of confession, an object lesson in moral degeneration. Once embarked on her life of crime, her career becomes a case study in the obsessive accumulation of wealth for its own sake. The amassing of possessions becomes an end in itself, justifying theft, duplicity and immorality in its pursuit. Moll is always willing to justify her behaviour to herself and her readers and becomes adept at rationalising it.

Considerable critical debate has focused on the genuineness or otherwise of Moll's reformation. As she expresses it, it seems real enough:

> It was now that for the first time I felt any real signs of
> Repentance; I now began to look back upon my past Life with
> abhorrence, and having a kind of view into the other Side of
> time, the things of Life, as I believe they do with every Body at
> such a time, began to look a different Aspect, and quite another
> Shape, than they did before.   (p. 287)

There can be no question that she convinces *herself* of the reality
of her transformation, but whether the reader shares her conviction
is open to doubt. A serious criticism which can be levelled at the
novel is that Moll is a static figure, that she remains fundamentally
unchanged throughout her experiences and simply responds to
events as they unfold. Those who hold this view maintain that as a
character she is inherently unscrupulous and that her final conver-
sion is unconvincing and contrived. Equally strong arguments can
be adduced to support the opposite view: that Moll is misguided
but not fundamentally wicked and that her repentance in the
prison is genuine. There is no mistaking the eloquence of her con-
version (pp. 287–92) nor the intensity of her emotions on confess-
ing her past crimes to the Minister – 'This honest friendly way of
treating me, unlocked all the Sluices of my Passions: He broke into
my very Soul by it; and I unravelled all the Wickedness of my Life
to him' (p. 288). It is worth reminding ourselves that Defoe *had* to
have an ending in which Moll is a reformed character: without this
he would have laid himself open to the charge that *Moll Flanders* is
simply a catalogue of crime and salacity. Given that this conclusion
was forced upon him by the nature of his material, one cannot but
admire his artistry in achieving it. Her change of heart, regret for
her past actions and success in attaining ultimate contentment form
the most satisfying part of the novel. When she unburdens herself
to the Minister ('I gave him an Abridgement of this whole History; I
gave him the Picture of my Conduct for 50 Years in Miniature') she
is presenting him in effect with a summation of the novel. *Moll
Flanders,* then, is both a realistic novel and a confession in which
she lays bare her soul for the judgement of her audience.

Closely linked to the debate over her reformation is the argument
concerning Defoe's use of irony. Is the story intended to be read as a
straightforward narrative comparable with *Joseph Andrews* or *Tom
Jones,* or is the entire work an ironic fable? To put the question in a
different way: does Defoe intend his readers to take Moll's story at
face value or is he well aware of her duplicity and intends us to

take her story as a case study in self-delusion? My own reading supports Ian Watt's contention that 'there is certainly nothing in *Moll Flanders* which clearly indicates that Defoe sees the story differently from the heroine'.[47] Clearly, he intended his readers to see Moll warts and all: to see her as a fallible human being subject to the normal temptations and to follow her in her journey through life, sharing in her misfortunes and happinesses. Unquestionably there is a large element of comedy in her story. In the early scenes in particular Moll is preoccupied with love, sexuality and marriage, and sees in these abundant scope for earthy humour. The episode in which she is afraid her first husband will detect that she is not a virgin (pp. 56–8) is characteristic of many in a kind of coy bawdiness, a circumlocution that anticipates the style of Fielding's *Shamela* or the conversations between the widow Wadman and Uncle Toby in Sterne's *Tristram Shandy*. Clearly, both Moll and her creator saw in sex, courtship and marriage an area for comedy which is entertaining without being in any way pornographic. *Moll Flanders* is a world removed from John Cleland's *Fanny Hill* (1749). Moll shies away from explicitness; she is content to convey her meaning through evasion and innuendo.

For all his plodding, pedestrian style and apparent lack of sophistication Defoe remains a curiously modern writer in his fascination with moral ambiguity. Moll is an inconsistent character in that she is neither wholly good nor wholly bad and that the motives for her actions are often a mixture of selfishness and compassion. In her ambivalence she anticipates the characters of Stevenson – most notably John Silver in *Treasure Island* and the Durie brothers in *The Master of Ballantrae*. In creating her and imbuing her with life, Defoe is in effect laying before us a sample of human life in all its diversity. To contemplate her story is inevitably to call into question whether there are universally applicable moral laws, whether all actions are inherently right or wrong. It is precisely because Moll is a complex mixture of greed and altruism that she holds our interest throughout her adventures; we recognise in her the matrix from which countless men and women are borne.

But the book is unresolved in the sense that Defoe's attitude to his heroine remains ultimately in doubt. Through all the vicissitudes of her life her reactions are totally utilitarian; she displays little imagination and scant concern for the feelings of those she defrauds. Does Defoe approve or disapprove of her behaviour? And what does he intend his readers' attitude to be? It is evident that Moll possesses qualities which many readers would identify with and admire. She is tough, resourceful, a woman of spirit and determination. At the same time she possesses less-desirable attributes: her obsession with money and status, her self-centredness, her unscrupulous behaviour in pursuing her own ends. Are these qualities which Defoe shared? One of the weaknesses of the novel is arguably that there is too little distance between author and narrator; that in having as his central character a woman preoccupied with the accumulation of wealth, Defoe was simply extolling attitudes he himself regarded as unexceptional.

On the face of it, Moll is an extremely unattractive character. She is on her own admission a liar, a thief, a petty criminal and a whore. Yet so vividly does Defoe imbue her with life that the reader identifies with her in her quest for happiness, and admires her toughness and intelligence in the face of all manner of misfortunes. She is a much more solid, rounded character than Captain Singleton, for example, and displays qualities of resilience and hard-headedness which gain our sympathy. Not the least remarkable feature of the novel is Defoe's ability to reach inside her mind, to see her emotions and thought processes and convey these to the reader in a totally convincing way. The novel is dominated by her personality, by her resourcefulness and resilience in her journey through life.

On the other hand, it can be argued that critical debate concerning authorial intention regarding *Moll Flanders* is finally irrelevant, that Defoe is content simply to present a detailed account of the realities of a particular life and leave his readers to form their own conclusions. Those who hold this view maintain that the reader is confronted with a choice – either *Moll Flanders* is a moral fable, a parable on the theme of degeneration and redemption, or it has no moral and is simply an attempt to present a specimen human life. Which of these views one adopts will depend not only on the story itself but on the preconceptions one brings to it.

Behind Moll's life of pretence there is, of course, a much larger pretence: that the story before us is a truthful autobiographical account narrated by an infamous woman criminal. Defoe's skill in creating the illusion of reality is such that the reader has forcibly to remind himself that this is indeed an illusion and that the book is a work of fiction. To illustrate the point let us take the incident when Moll, newly married and staying at an inn, looks out of the window and sees to her dismay her former husband:

the great Room of the House look'd into the Street, and my new
Spouse being below Stairs, I had walk'd to the end of the Room,
and it being a pleasant warm Day, I had opened the Window,
and was standing at it for some Air, when I saw three Gentlemen
come by on Horseback and go into an Inn just against us.

It was not to be conceal'd, nor was it so doubtful as to leave
me any room to question it, but the second of the three was my
Lancashire Husband: I was frighted to Death, I never was in
such a Consternation in my Life, I thought I should have sunk
into the Ground, my Blood run Chill in my Veins, and I trembl'd
as if I had been in a cold Fit of an Ague: I say there was no room
to question the Truth of it, I knew his Cloaths, I knew his Horse,
and I knew his Face.   (p. 185)

Unquestionably, this has the feel of reality: 'I knew his Cloaths, I
knew his Horse, and I knew his Face.' The reader would have to
make a conscious effort to grasp the truth that neither Moll nor her
Lancashire husband have any solidity, that neither has any existence
outside the words on the page. Yet Defoe in a single paragraph has
etched the scene indelibly before us. The narrator's assertion of its
actuality – 'I say there was no room to question the Truth of it' – is so
disarming as to carry conviction. An equally striking example of the
technique occurs a few pages later when Moll is first tempted into an
act of theft. The scene is described in unforgettably vivid terms:

I dress'd me, for I had still pretty good Cloaths, and went out: I
am very sure I had no manner of Design in my Head, when I
went out, I neither knew or considered where to go, or on what
Business; but as the Devil carried me out and laid his Bait for me,
so he brought me to be sure to the place, for I knew not whither I
was going or what I did.

Wandring thus about I knew not whither, I pass'd by an
Apothecary's Shop in Leadenhall-street, where I saw Lye on a
Stool just before the Counter, a little Bundle wrapt in a white
Cloth; beyond it, stood a maid Servant with her Back to it,
looking up towards the top of the Shop, where the Apothecary's
Apprentice, as I suppose, was standing up on the Counter, with
his Back also to the Door, and a Candle in his Hand, looking and
reaching up to the upper Shelf for something he wanted, so that
both were engag'd mighty earnestly, and no Body else in the
Shop.

This was the Bait; and the Devil who I said laid the Snare, as readily prompted me, as if he had spoke, for I remember, and shall never forget it, 'twas like a Voice spoken to me over my Shoulder, take the Bundle; be quick; do it this Moment; it was no sooner said but I step'd into the Shop, and with my Back to the Wench, as if I had stood up for a Cart that was going by, I put my Hand behind me and took the Bundle, and went off with it, the Maid or the Fellow not perceiving me, or any one else.

(pp. 191–2)

The vignette has the clarity of a Pre-Raphaelite painting. As frequently happens in Defoe's fiction, the episode is prefaced by an insistence on its randomness: 'I knew not whither I was going or what I did.' This is followed by precise details of location – the name of the street and the type of shop – and a highly circumstantial description of the shop's interior. The latter, so detailed as to resemble stage directions, fixes the scene with the precision of a photograph. We are told where the maid and apprentice are standing and the direction they are facing. When Moll then hears a voice over her shoulder: 'take the Bundle; be quick; do it this Moment', it is as if the reader also hears the voice and shares her moment of temptation. The theft is immediately followed by flight and remorse:

It is impossible to express the Horror of my Soul all the while I did it: When I went away I had no heart to run, or scarce to mend my pace; I cross'd the Street indeed, and went down the first turning I came to, and I think it was a Street that went thro' into Fenchurch-street, from thence I cross'd and turn'd thro' so many ways and turning that I could never tell which way it was, nor where I went, for I felt not the Ground, I stept on, and the farther I was out of Danger, the faster I went, till tyr'd and out of Breath, I was forc'd to sit down on a little Bench at a Door, and then I began to recover, and found I was got into Thames-street near Billingsgate: I rested me a little and went on, my Blood was all in a Fire, my Heart beat as if I was in sudden Fright: In short, I was under such a Surprize that I still knew not whither I was a going, or what to do.

After I had try'd my self thus with walking a long way about, and so eagerly, I began to consider and make home to my Lodging, where I came about Nine a Clock at Night. (p. 192)

Again we note the characteristic Defoe touches: 'It is impossible to express the Horror of my Soul all the while I did it'; 'I had no Heart to run, or scarce to mend my pace'; 'I felt not the Ground I stept on'. Reading this passage it is impossible to doubt Moll's breathlessness, her fear, her confused feelings. An awareness of the storyteller as a living, breathing human being is inescapable. Another pleasing touch is that after all the twistings and turnings of her flight, she pauses to rest in a street she identifies: 'Thames-street near Billingsgate'. This is followed by a return to rationality – 'I began to consider' – and a safe journey back to her lodging 'about Nine a Clock at Night'. The entire episode of the stealing and the panic-stricken journey possesses many touches we have come to identify with Defoe: precise details of time and place, pictorial clarity of description, a powerful sense of immediacy and involvement, and an overriding impression of reality. Added to these is an insight into the narrator's thoughts and motives that is engaging in its frankness. It is as if Moll is anxious to conceal nothing, to be completely open with the reader, even at the risk of incrimination: 'I am very sure I had no manner of Design in my Head, when I went out'; 'This was the Bait; and the Devil who I said laid the Snare, as readily prompted me'; 'I still knew not whither I was a going, or what to do'. The style seems so plain and straightforward that it is easy to miss the sense of an authorial presence; the story seems to tell itself. This is itself an illusion, for behind each episode is a controlling intelligence guiding and shaping the narrative.

In seeking to account for the novel's continuing popularity over a period of 250 years we return again and again to the intimate relationship between narrator and reader, a bond reminiscent of that achieved by Dickens in *David Copperfield*. An example of this is Moll's habit of talking directly to the reader: 'It is enough to tell you', 'so you may give me leave to speak of myself', 'you may easily see it was all nature', 'all this, you may be sure, was as I wished'. This tendency to address the reader conversationally, as if taking him into her confidence, establishes a close bond between reader and text which strengthens the illusion of veracity.

The novel is an impressive achievement in its own right and reveals Defoe's growing self-confidence in the handling of dialogue and incident. Consider, for example, the conversation between Moll and her lover (pp. 36–40) or between Moll and her would-be husband James (pp. 134–8), in which there is a vigorous cut and thrust of opposing arguments. These are not stylised conversations between cardboard characters, as occasionally take place in the earlier novels, but realistic exchanges between living people. We are even privy to her secret thoughts, as when she asks James outright to divorce his wife:

> Well, Sir, says I, then you must Divorce her; if you can prove what you say, you may certainly get that done, and then, I suppose, you are free.
> That's very tedious and expensive, says he.
> Why, says I, if you can get any Woman you like to take your word, I suppose your Wife would not dispute the Liberty with you that she takes herself.
> Ay, says he, but 'twou'd be hard to bring a honest Woman to do that; and for the other sort, says he, I have had enough of her to meddle with any more Whores.
> It occurr'd to me presently, I would have taken your word with all my Heart, if you had but ask'd me the Question, but that was to my self; to him I reply'd why you shut the Door against any honest Woman accepting you, for you condemn all that should venture upon you at once, and conclude, that really a Woman that takes you now, can't be honest.   (p. 136)

At the end of this dialogue Moll confides to the reader: 'I played with this lover as an angler does with a trout.' It is episodes of this kind in which characters do not simply talk to one another but suppress their thoughts, acknowledge their duplicity – 'My heart said yes to this offer at first word, but it was necessary to play the hypocrite a little more with him' – that convince us that in *Moll Flanders* we are witnessing the birth of the novel as an art form. Humour, irony, realism and perception are present in abundance.

Is the novel merely a collection of disparate episodes or is there an overall design? The fact that Moll is born in Newgate prison and experiences her repentance there gives the work a superficial unity, as does her final reunion and attainment of happiness with her Lancashire husband. But it is Moll's life and personality that provide the essential core of the work; it is the story of her development, career and repentance which form its substance.

Defoe's biographer James Sutherland has pointed out that 'Much as he loved to instruct, he loved even more to contemplate human life, to watch the progress of a human soul, the ebb and flow of worldly prosperity.'[48] Defoe was fascinated by conduct, by the drives which motivate behaviour and the accidents of chance and fortune that shape our lives. *Moll Flanders* is a shapeless novel, in the sense that its only unifying element is the character of Moll herself, but he was seeking to render the chaos of life rather than a neatly structured work of art in the vein of Jane Austen or Henry James. In this regard the novel is far more akin to the loose autobiographical narratives of Dickens and Wells than to works of classical perfection. James took Wells to task for his fondness for the genre, asserting that the form sacrifices perspective and 'puts a premium on the loose, the improvised, the cheap and the easy'.[49] Given Defoe's gift for reaching inside the personalities of his central characters and his intention to present a sample human life in all its rich variety it is difficult to see how else he could have told the story. For him what mattered was the panorama of Moll's life: her journey through innocence, maturity, degeneration and redemption, and the lessons she has learned from her experiences. It is surely to this that he is drawing attention when he remarks in the Preface: 'it is to be hoped that such readers will be much more pleased with the Moral, than the Fable; with the Application, than with the Relation, and with the End of the Writer, than with the Life of the Person written of'.

In her tendency to self-delusion, her shifting moods, her alternations between selfishness and concern for others, and above all in her ambivalent moral stance, Moll is an amalgam of human attributes. This, Defoe says in effect, is a case study in behaviour: what are we to make of it? It is true that there is little in the novel in the way of development or resolution; Moll remains much the same at the end as she was at the beginning. But in approaching *Moll Flanders*, or indeed any Defoe novel, the reader must be wary of bringing to it perceptions derived from a long-established novelistic tradition. Defoe was writing 90 years before the publication of Austen's *Pride and Prejudice* and 150 years before the publication of Hardy's *Under the Greenwood Tree*. He was still feeling his way in a new and untried art form. One can only applaud the heroism of his endeavour to depict a vibrant central figure who embodies the competing tensions and contradictions of his age.

A Journal of the Plague Year

A Journal of the Plague Year, published in 1722, can claim with some justification to be the first historical novel in the English language. Its title-page proclaims it to be 'Observations or Memorials of the most Remarkable Occurences, as well Public as Private, which happened in London during the last Great Visitation in 1665: Written by a Citizen who continued all the while in London'. Defoe was such a skilful journalist that he succeeds in creating an illusion of authenticity, so much so that many contemporary readers accepted the *Journal* at face value as an eye-witness account written at the time of the Great Plague. Even today it is easy to make the same mistake, lulled by Defoe's expertise as a literary counterfeiter into a total suspension of disbelief.

A moment's reflection will demonstrate that the book cannot be what it purports to be. The Great Plague of London took place in 1665, when Defoe was five years of age. Though he may well have had vivid memories of sights and sounds of the time, and his parents and relatives almost certainly told him their recollections – such a traumatic event must have been a topic of conversation for many years afterwards, a child of that age cannot have witnessed the Plague with the intensity of detail evinced in the *Journal*. In any event it seems probable that Defoe was evacuated from London for the duration of the epidemic. We know that he had an uncle named Henry Foe who was, like Defoe's narrator 'H. F.', a Whitechapel saddler (he died in 1674) and it seems likely that the *Journal* is based in part on his reminiscences. It is therefore important to understand what the *Journal* is and what it is not. Despite all indications to the contrary, it is not what it appears to be: a contemporary account written by a single observer who personally witnessed the events he describes. It is, rather, an imaginative reconstruction based partly on Defoe's memories, partly on accounts passed to him in later years by relatives and friends, and partly on written sources such as *The Weekly Bills of Mortality* and Nathaniel Hodges's contemporary report *Loimologia*. In common with Orwell's *Down and Out in Paris and London*, it is a literary re-creation of events and anecdotes culled from a variety of sources and woven into a coherent and vivid narrative.

But a mere hoax – comparable to Poe's accounts of an ascent to the moon or a crossing of the Atlantic by balloon – would not have attained the status enjoyed today by *A Journal of the Plague Year*. It is widely acknowledged as one of the most compelling accounts of disaster in all literature and has exercised a seminal influence on the novel of survival. What gives the book its distinctive quality is its extraordinary air of veracity and the apparent ease with which Defoe evokes the feel of a city in the grip of calamity. Its apparent lack of literary pretension is deceptive. Anthony Burgess has said of Defoe that 'his novels are too much novels to seem like novels; they read like real life'. He adds: 'The art is too much concealed to seem like art and hence the art is frequently discounted.'[50]

The *Journal* abounds in phrases designed to convince the reader that the narrator is describing scenes and incidents witnessed with his own eyes. Expressions such as 'There was one unhappy Citizen, *within my Knowledge*', 'This was a most grievous and afflicting thing to me, *who saw it all from my own Windows*', 'In these walks *I had many dismal Scenes before my Eyes*', 'I remember, and while I am writing this Story *I think I hear the very Sound of it*' create an atmosphere of truthfulness and immediacy. The reader has a sense of involvement, of being a participant in an authentic contemporary narrative. Continually, H. F. employs phrases suggesting personal knowledge: 'there were innumerable Instances of it, and I could name several in my Neighborhood'; 'one family... not far from me'; 'I was indeed shocked with this Sight'; 'It often pierc'd my very Soul to hear the Groans and Crys of those who were thus tormented'. There is a powerful sense of H. F. as an honest authorial voice, at pains to establish the truth of a disaster which at times overwhelms him in its horror. he emerges as a character in his own right, compassionate, sceptical and judicial, determined to convey the magnitude of a disaster almost beyond his understanding.

The tone is established from the first sentence: 'It was about the Beginning of September 1664, that I, among the Rest of my Neighbours, heard in ordinary Discourse, that the Plague was returned again in Holland....' These opening words, at once calm and portentous, lead to an introductory survey of the epidemic, outlining its outbreak and growth parish by parish and the insidious spread of rumour and alarm. The apparently casual phrase 'I, among the Rest of my Neighbours' immediately established H. F. as one of a number of eye-witnesses who can personally testify to the truth of their account. The words 'heard in ordinary Discourse' are a reminder that Defoe was writing in an age when news was passed on by word of mouth; he goes on to add: 'We had no such thing as printed News Papers in those Days, to spread Rumours and Reports of Things.' Living today in an age of instant communication it is difficult for us to comprehend a world in which news of disasters was conveyed on foot or horseback, and rumour and falsehood spread like wildfire.

Defoe interpolates his personal account with skilful use of tables and statistics tracing the course of the Plague. By referring to these tables one can gain an overview of the epidemic, following the number of deaths month by month, its geographical spread through London and the surrounding villages and the speed of its relentless advance. He had so much statistical information at his disposal that the *Journal* could easily have become a dry catalogue of mortality. Defoe avoids this trap through a deft interweaving of the general and the particular. A list of numbers of fatalities will be followed by personal anecdotes relating the account to individual cases: 'Passing thro' Token House Yard in Lothbury, of a sudden a Casement violently opened just over my Head'; 'Another encounter I had in the open day also'; 'I could give a great many such Stories as these, diverting enough, which in the long Course of that dismal Year, I met with.' This juxtaposition of the total picture and individual incidents is strikingly effective. The alternation of the overall situation with eye-witness accounts means that the reader never loses sight of the fact that the Plague was an immense tragedy, bringing pain, fear and death on a terrible scale. The casualties who people the narrative with horrifying regularity become real and human instead of a mere recital.

His anecdotes are so circumstantial and seemingly authentic as to add a solid dimension of realism to his account. There are numerous instances of this, of which the following is a characteristic example:

As I went along Houndsditch one Morning, about eight a Clock, there was a great Noise; it is true indeed, there was not much Crowd, because People were not very free to gather together, or to stay long together, when they were there, nor did I stay long there: But the Outcry was loud enough to prompt my Curiosity,

and I called to one that looked out of a Window, and asked what
was the Matter. (p. 48)

Many readers would pass this sentence by as unremarkable, but
Defoe's style merits close attention as an outstanding precursor of
the realist novel as exemplified by Dickens and Trollope. Note first
the precise sense of time and place, which gives an air of credibility
to the passage as a whole. Typically the narrator feels obliged to
explain why so few people were about, and also to assert that he
personally did not linger. He then goes on to say that 'the Outcry
was loud enough to prompt my Curiosity, and I called to one that
looked out of a Window'. This simple statement tells us much about
H. F. Despite the horror and anxiety of living in London at a time of
widespread epidemic he is not too preoccupied to have his interest
aroused by a noise, and to investigate. Even when surrounded by
death and upheaval he is anxious to find out what is the matter. It is
also characteristic of Defoe that the incident is described in a single
rambling sentence, as if the author is thinking aloud as he writes.
This conversational, discursive style – part description, part explanation – is so typical of his prose as to be a kind of trademark identifying his work. Through it all can be discerned a painstaking,
modest, plodding voice eager to convey to his audience a sense of
the universal disaster gripping the England he loves.

But the *Journal* is no mere agglomeration of facts and anecdotes.
The natural history of the Great Plague – its outbreak, spread and
decline – provides a logical structure for the book which Defoe
exploits to the full. In fact it did not end tidily at the end of 1665 but
continued well into the following year. We can forgive Defoe this
small poetic licence, for clearly he needed a conclusive ending for
his narrative. As it is, the book possesses a symmetry and cohesion
unusual in his fiction and reveals his growing self-confidence in the
handling of incident and dialogue. It is one of the most carefully
structured of all his works, for throughout his account he
consistently balances small incident against large-scale view, numer-
cal survey against graphic portrayal (see, for example, the description of the burial pit on pp. 59–63), personal experience against
objective summary.

At the exact mid-point of the *Journal* Defoe introduces the story
of three travellers who journey from London to Essex in an attempt
to avoid the worst of the contagion. His decision to place it in the
centre of the narrative suggests his recognition of its significance as

a turning point in his account and an object lesson in survival. With a novelist's sense of pacing he refers to the travellers, in passing as it were, much earlier in the book:

> I have by me a Story of two Brothers and their Kinsman, who being single Men, but that had stay'd in the City too long to get away, and indeed, not knowing where to go to have any Retreat, nor having wherewith to travel far, took a Course for their own Preservation.... The Story of those three Men, if the Reader will be content to have me give it in their own Persons, without taking upon me to either vouch the Particulars, or answer for any Mistakes, I shall give as distinctly as I can, believing the History will be a very good Pattern for any poor Man to follow.... (pp. 57–8)

Having whetted the reader's appetite in this way, Defoe does not come to the story itself for a further 60 pages, explaining: 'I say all this previous to the History, having yet, for the present, much more to say before I quit my own Part' (p. 58). The account of the wanderings and adventures of the three men – their occupations are baker, sail-maker and joiner (occupations chosen presumably for their ordinariness) – forms an exciting interlude and brings vividly to life the problems encountered by all those seeking to flee from the pestilence. Defoe clearly senses its importance for, while he is tempted to digress, he keeps returning to their adventures: 'This brings me back to the three poor Men', 'I come back to my three Men', 'But to return to my Travellers'. The debate between John the baker and Thomas the sail-maker whether to remain in London or flee forms a dramatic prelude to their journey (pp. 122–5) and is an interesting example of the author's skill in contrasting opposing points of view. When Thomas points out the difficulties inherent in any attempt to escape, John replies pertinently: 'there is no lying in the Street at such a Time as this; we had as good go into the Dead Cart at once: Therefore I say, if we stay here we are sure to die, and if we go away we can but die: I am resolved to be gone' (p. 124). There is no mistaking the force and eloquence of John's arguments. His plea that 'we had as good go into the Dead Cart at once', whereas if they flee they have at least a chance of survival, eventually convinces Thomas and the trio begin making plans for their journey.

Their wanderings through London, Kent and Essex enable Defoe to highlight the genuine fears of the villagers who are understandably reluctant to offer food or shelter to strangers, in case they are infected. The travellers also have to reckon with the strict vagrancy laws in force at that time which empowered magistrates to remove strangers and return them to their parish of origin. The travellers show considerable ingenuity in surmounting obstacles, obtaining food and devising temporary accommodation for themselves en route, including a series of tents, huts and sheds. The friendly rivalry between the sail-maker and the carpenter results in some artful contrivances for providing shelter. When they pitch their camp in Epping Forest, for example, the narrator observes that the carpenter constructed three huts made of poles, 'binding all the small ends together at the top, and thickening the sides with boughs of trees and bushes, so that they were completely close and warm' (p. 140). This Crusoe-like preoccupation with homely detail is characteristic of Defoe and adds a strong element of conviction to his story.

After many vicissitudes the wanderers join forces with another band of thirteen nomads and together they succeed in reaching Essex, from where they return to London after an absence of six months, the plague having by then greatly slackened. Defoe prefaces this interlude with the observation that 'Their Story has a Moral in every Part of it, and their whole Conduct, and that of some who joined with, is a Pattern for all poor Men to follow' (p. 122). The moral is surely that human ingenuity and resourcefulness are at their keenest when survival is at stake and that man is justified in employing improvisation, artifice, even subterfuge, rather than succumb to extinction. Here, as in *Robinson Crusoe* and *Captain Singleton,* Defoe's overriding concern is survival in the face of a hostile environment. Man, he suggests, must deploy his reason to overcome difficulties and escape from calamity. When the wanderers are confronted with hostility of fear they respond with coolness: 'John argued very calmly with them a great while'; 'John wrought so upon the Townsmen by taking thus rationally and smoothly to them, that they went away.' Their triumph is not simply a victory over the plague but over bigotry, resentment and officialdom. It is also a triumph over all manner of natural obstacles including hunger, fatigue, cold and wet. Throughout their adventures the travellers have to contend with humour and counter-rumour warning of the rapid spread of the disease, and need to amend their plans continually to take stock of conflicting reports. That they prevail over every setback through their own resourcefulness is a heartening vindication of the human spirit.

The *Journal, then, is at once a fictional reconstruction of the London of 1665 and an allegory of the ceaseless quest for survival.* In a deeper sense it is a fable on the unpredictable nature of existence and the power of the irrational. For the Plague stands for all that is irrational and inexplicable in nature; H. F., with his reasonable approach and methodicalness, for the human instinct to impose order on chaos. The narrator's attempt to impose a rational explanation on a contagion which in the last analysis cannot be explained is the central contradiction of the book. The Plague is beyond reason, beyond the control of the human will. When he declares 'the Power of man was baffled, and brought to an End' (p. 35) it is a cry from the heart. In the face of calamity on such a scale it is small wonder, he tells us, that so many Londoners took refuge in despair or flight. He himself, for all his apparent calm, is not immune from despondency. At the height of the Plague a confession is wrung from him: 'I must acknowledge that this time was Terrible, that I was sometimes at the End of all my Resolutions, and that I had not the Courage that I had at the Beginning' (p. 177). This reminder of his humanity strengthens rather than diminishes his credibility. It is a reminder that, like Crusoe, H. F. is a fallible human being who is not afraid to acknowledge his shortcomings. He has carefully established the persona of a man of reason who is sitting in his study many years after the Plague to write a distillation of all he has seen and heard. But he is forced to confess that there were times when he was at the end of his tether, moments of black uncertainty when he gave way to despair.

Above all, the *Journal* is a novel of London, rich in topographical detail and powerfully evoking the atmosphere of the capital city of the mid-seventeenth century. The accumulation of geographical detail strengthens the effect of veracity achieved by a narrative so fertile in incident. An interesting example of the technique is the account of the journey from Wapping to Bow:

> But then a Difficulty came in their Way, that as they set out from the hither end of Wapping near the Hermitage, and that the Plague was now very Violent, especially on the North side of the City, as in Shoreditch and Cripplegate Parish, they did not think it safe for them to go near those Parts; so they went away East through Radcliff High-way, as far as Radcliff-Cross, and leaving Stepney Church still on their Left-hand, being afraid to come up

from Radcliff-Cross to Mile-End, because they must come just by the Church-yard, and because the Wind that seemed to blow more from the West, blow'd directly from the side of the City where the Plague was hottest. So I say, leaving Stepney, they fetched a long Compass, and going to Poplar and Bromley, came into the great Road just at Bow.   (p. 128)

One notes the continual reference to circumstantial detail: 'the hither end of Wapping near the Hermitage'; 'leaving Stepney Church still on their Left-hand'; 'because they must come just by the Church-yard'; 'they fetched a long Compass, and going to Poplar and Bromley, came into the great Road just at Bow'. When the reader is confronted by identifiable locations that can be traced on a map the illusion of verisimilitude is inevitably heightened. One is reminded of the narrator's journey from Leatherhead to Woking in H. G. Wells's *The War of the Worlds* or the solitary walk from Fulham to Primrose Hill in the same novel.

Defoe had, of course, many years of experience as a journalist before he wrote fiction, and had acquired considerable facility in the use of language. He was familiar with the techniques which add authenticity to a description: the accumulation of circumstantial detail; the seemingly casual introduction of corroborative material; the deliberate understatement to heighten impact. As an example of the latter, consider the following sentence: 'the Terror was so great at last, that the Courage of the People appointed to carry away the Dead, began to fail them; nay, several of them died altho' they had the Distemper before, and were recover'd' (p. 179). Plain statements of this kind are far more effective in communicating the horror of the plague than a wealth of verbosity. The assertion that 'the Courage of the People...began to fail them' is moving in its simplicity.

It could be said of *A Journal of the Plague Year* that London is the central character, as it is of Dickens's *Little Dorrit* or Wells's *Tono-Bungay*. In a wider sense it can be regarded, in common with them, as a 'Condition of England' novel, an epic offering a panoramic view of London in a time of crisis.[51] In a localised world in which three-quarters of the population lived in villages and the population of London was half-a-million, it must have been difficult to obtain an overview of the total situation. The *Journal* brilliantly provides this. The reader is, as it were, suspended in a balloon above the city, watching the ebb and flow of the plague, seeing the people hurrying to and fro and the rise and fall of hope. Consider, for example, the unforgettable description of the beginning of the end:

> It is impossible to express the Change that appear'd in the very Countenances of the People, that Thursday Morning, when the Weekly Bill came out; it might have been perceived in their Countenances, that a secret Surprize and Smile of Joy sat on every Bodies Face; they shook one another by the Hands in the Streets, who would hardly go on the same Side of the way with one another before; where the Streets were not too broad, they would open their Windows and call from one House to another, and ask'd how they did, and if they had heard the good News, that the Plague was abated.   (p. 245)

Defoe succeeds very well in conveying the camaraderie borne of a disaster shared by all – 'they shook one another by the Hands in the Streets'. One is reminded irresistibly of accounts of the London blitz of 1940. There is the same sense of a universal calamity from which no one is immune, of a shared reprieve, of good news passing by word of mouth. Overriding all these elements is a sense of community, of the English under adversity: a normally reticent population asking each other 'how they did' and speaking to strangers for the first time. Seen in this light the book seems a remarkably prescient account of civilisation under stress and a striking anticipation of the impact of war on modern cities.

A Journal of the Plague Year has inspired a multitude of imitations, most notably Camus's *The Plague* (1947), and can be seen as a pre-cursor of the disaster novel exemplified by *The War of the Worlds*, Jack London's *The Scarlet Plague*, John Wyndham's *The Day of the Triffids* and John Christopher's *The Death of Grass*. It shares with these a preoccupation with survival, with the story of an individual or group of individuals using their ingenuity in order to survive against a breakdown of civilisation. There is an overwhelming sense of calamity as the narrator struggles to convey the full impact of the awesome sights he describes: 'Sorrow and Sadness sat upon every Face'; 'the Power of Man was baffled, and brought to an End'; [Death now began not, as we may say, to hover over every ones Head only, but to look into their Houses, and Chambers, and stare in their Faces] 'and a great many that went thither Sound, brought Death Home with them'. This determination to convey the horror of a disaster almost beyond comprehension rises to a climax of unbearable intensity as the narrator describes a desolate London in the grip of the Plague:

> It is here, however, to be observ'd, that after the Funerals became so many, that People could not Toll the Bell, Mourn, or Weep, or wear Black for one another, as they did before; no, nor so much as make Coffins for those that died; so after a while the fury of the Infection appeared to be so éncreased, that in short, they shut up no Houses at all; it seem'd enough that all the Remedies of that Kind had been used till they were found fruitless, and that the Plague spread itself with an irresistible Fury, so that, as the Fire the succeeding Year, spread itself and burnt with such Violence, that the Citizens in Despair, gave over their Endeavours to extinguish it, so in the Plague, it came at last to such Violence that the People sat still looking at one another, and seem'd quite abandon'd to Despair; whole Streets seem'd to be desolated, and not to be shut up only, but to be emptied of their Inhabitants; Doors were left open, Windows stood shattering with the Wind in empty Houses, for want of People to shut them: In a Word, People began to give up themselves to their Fears, and to think that all regulations and Methods were in vain, and that there was nothing to be hoped for, but an universal Desolation. (pp. 170–1)

The passage is filled with memorable images: the inability of people to toll the bell or make coffins for the dead; their growing despair in the face of overwhelming tragedy; the desolation of a London empty and abandoned; the apparent hopelessness of a population reconciled to destruction. Most striking of all is the statement that 'Doors were left open, Windows stood shattering with the Wind in empty Houses, for want of People to shut them'. So powerful is this image that it lingers in the mind long after the book has been read, a vivid anticipation of the scenes of urban ruin produced by modern warfare.[52] It is in such passages that Defoe rises beyond the calm, dispassionate persona he is at such pains to present and reaches an eloquence matching his apocalyptic theme. There can be few English writers who have depicted in such unforgettable terms the nightmare of 'universal desolation'.

The passage is characteristic of Defoe not only in its graphic use of fact ('nor so much as make Coffins for those that died') and haunting detail ('it came at last to such Violence that the People sat still looking at one another') but its dual perspective. Throughout the *Journal* the narrator is looking back on events occurring in the past and presenting a story that is unfolding as he writes. To achieve both points of view simultaneously is no easy task, but H. F. is in such command of his material that he succeeds at one and the same time in unfolding a gripping narrative and placing it in a historical and social context. The casually inserted phrase 'as the Fire the succeeding Year, spread itself and burnt with such Violence' introduces at once a note of hindsight; clearly these words cannot have been written in 1665. But they heighten immensely the impact of the paragraph, for they lead directly to a comparison between the Plague and the Fire: 'the Citizens in Despair, gave over their Endeavours to extinguish it, so in the Plague ... the People ... seem'd quite abandon'd to Despair'.

The danger is always to underestimate Defoe, for though he wrote at great speed and seems to have revised his work as he went along, he was by no means a careless or unpainstaking writer. The *Journal* as a whole is impressive testimony to his ability to weld a large mass of material into a coherent and readable narrative, while never losing sight of the fact that he is writing a novel and not a treatise.

It is in its descriptions of a community decimated by forces beyond human control, a community beset by fear and resignation, that the *Journal* has exercised such a profound effect on the modern novel, most notably on the work of Wells and Orwell. What Wells termed civilisation 'losing coherency, losing shape and efficiency, guttering, softening, running at last in that swift liquefaction of the social body'[53] is the same process H. F. is describing in his account of London laid waste by pestilence. In the description of 'Dead London' in *The War of the Worlds* or the account of a populace numbed by endless war in *Nineteen Eighty-Four* can be seen Defoe's potent influence. There is the same sense of a people struggling to come to terms with disaster, contriving against all odds to maintain a semblance of order and normality. There is above all a sense of civilisation under strain, of law breaking down in the face of anarchy. Beyond this both Wells and Orwell learned much from Defoe in fashioning a style of reportage that is neither a conventional novel nor a work of non-fiction but a hybrid of the two. *Tono-Bungay* and *The Road to Wigan Pier*, for example, both contain a skilful blending of fiction and sociological comment; both are rich in incident yet provide an overview of England at a particular point in time; both use the device of an autobiographical narrator who comments on all he sees and attempts to interpret his world for the benefit of his readers. Malcolm Bradbury has credited Wells with creating a new type of novel, 'a novel of deliberate contingency based on the fluidity of the autobiographic narrator'.[54] Defoe's first-person narratives can be seen as archetypes of this style of writing, fusing in a coherent whole the imaginative curiosity of the novelist and the methodicalness of the sociologist. *A Journal of the Plague Year* provides a snapshot of England at a traumatic moment of history. In choosing the Plague as his theme Defoe embraced a 'commanding centre' which both justifies his novel in Jamesian terms and provided him with a dramatic fable ideally suited to his talents.

Colonel Jack

Colonel Jack inevitably invites comparison with *Moll Flanders*. Both novels are dominated by a central character who embarks on a life of crime and finds happiness and success in Virginia, both purport to be autobiographical narratives looking back on past misdeeds, and both depict a fallible storyteller rising from humble beginnings to wealth through a combination of ingenuity and courage. The similarities are, however, more superficial than real. The moral ambiguity which forms such a pervasive element in *Moll Flanders* is almost totally absent from *Colonel Jack*, for Jack is a far less ambivalent figure. What drives him in his journey through life is his determination to be a gentleman.

On the first page Jack tells us that his mother was a gentlewoman, and that his father's admonition to her was 'always take care to bid me *remember, that I was a Gentleman*' (Defoe's italics). When, later, he embarks on a career as a thief he is smitten with remorse for his actions, confiding: 'and now it came into my head with a double force, that this was the High Road to the Devil, and that certainly this was not the Life of a Gentleman!' (p. 67). Years afterwards, when he has severed himself from criminal activities, he returns to this theme with renewed force:

> That Original something, I knew not what, that used formerly to Check me in the first meannesses of my Youth, and us'd to Dictate to me when I was but a Child, that I was to be a Gentleman, continued to Operate upon me now, in a manner I cannot Describe.... (p. 155)

The aspiration to be a gentleman provides him with an *idée fixe* which is never far from the surface of the novel. The story is in large measure a search for moral values, the narrative of a well-meaning and caring young man who is resolved to gain control of his own life. At first he is without standards – as he expresses it: 'I had, I say, all the way hitherto, no manner of thoughts about the Good or Evil of what I was embarked in' (p. 60) – but simultaneously is troubled by scruples: 'I had a strange kind of uninstructed Conscience at that Time'(p. 55). The series of false starts which form the substance of his adventures can be regarded as case studies in dependence: each is a variation on the theme of master and servant, teacher and pupil. Whether his master is Will (petty crime), Mr Smith (farming) or the Chevalier (soldiering), Jack's life is essentially one of aspiration and growing self-respect. Through his acumen and intelligence he works out his own salvation and gains mastery of his nature.

The master – servant theme is inverted when others in turn become dependent on Jack. The negro Mouchat becomes utterly loyal to him and treats him as if he were a god. His first wife, though initially unfaithful, is finally reconciled to him and by the end of the story is totally reliant on his compassion. When he reflects at the conclusion of his narrative that 'the History of Men's Lives may be many ways made Useful, and Instructing to those who read them' (p. 307), we are left to draw the inference that Jack has shed his dependence on others and learned to become master of his own destiny. Jack's final discovery is of himself.

Colonel Jack displays some signs of being hastily written. Defoe simply dismisses the hero's journey from Scotland to Virginia – a voyage lasting four weeks – in a single line: 'Nothing material happened to me during the voyage', and there are places where a gap of several years is bridged in a few words: 'In this private condition I continued about two year more'. The chronology of the story is also erratic in contrast to the carefully worked out time-scale of *Moll Flanders*. Yet despite this, it is a much more *controlled* novel than *Moll*, a story dominated by a single image: Jack's journey from innocence to maturity.

In the opening sentence Jack describes his life as 'a Checquer Work of Nature' and confesses that he is now able 'to look back upon it from a safer Distance'. Seen as the story of Jack's discovery of his own nature the novel can be regarded as a primitive *Bildungsroman*, a first essay in handling the kind of raw material from which *Oliver Twist* and *David Copperfield* were hewn more than a century later. Much of its fascination, as with Defoe's earlier fictions, lies in the writer's ability to reach inside the mind of his narrator and to adopt the tone of a man of experience looking back on a wayward child. When Jack describes himself as 'a poor innocent boy', for example, he adds the words 'and (as I remember, my very Thoughts perfectly well) I had no Evil in my Intentions' (p. 19). The phrase in parenthesis is a reminder of this dual perspective: that the narrator is simultaneously the inexperienced youth and the self-made man looking back on his boyhood self. Jack's gradual development of a moral sense and his deeply rooted desire to become a gentleman give a sense of movement to the novel as a whole, an upward-striving towards standards of behaviour befitting a man of honour. On the title page he describes himself as 'truly honourable': an indication of his conception of himself as a man of integrity. For all his aspirations he remains throughout an ordinary person subject to the normal human failings – there are many occasions when he displays self-doubt, prevarication or diffidence in spite of his urge towards nobler qualities. It is largely for this reason and the fact that Jack learns from his misfortunes as well as his successes that he engages the reader's sympathy. His progression towards security and happiness is achieved despite many buffetings of ill-judgement and weakness.

Not only is it a *Bildungsroman* remarkable for its insight into the mind of a child but one of the earliest sentimental novels, a genre that became extremely popular in the eighteenth century, especially after Sterne's *A Sentimental Journey* (1768). During one of Jack's many pauses to take stock of his life and attitudes, he remarks a propos of his mental and material development: 'Now I found differing Sentiments of things taking Place in my Mind' (p. 155), and goes on to express his 'secret horror at things passed'. The word 'Sentiments' is suggestive in this connection and is an interesting indication of Jack's emotional response to life and conduct. Consider the affecting scene in which he seeks out a woman he has robbed and makes recompense for his theft (pp. 84–7). The scene abounds in the language of emotion: 'grief', 'tears', 'touched', 'moved', 'wept'. It is genuinely heartbreaking in its intensity, with no hint of the duplicity or cynicism which occasionally disfigures Moll's narrative. Many times he has reproached himself with his callousness in robbing her: 'my Heart had reproached me many a time with that cruel Action' (p. 83). The frequent references to the heart as the source of feelings, the continual references to weeping, and abundant evidence of the hero's sensitivity all confirm *Colonel Jack* as a novel rich in sentiment.

As a hero Jack is naturally good, a man incapable of a mean or hurtful action. Defoe seems to have intended that the story be regarded as a parable rather than a truthful account, a point he makes clear in the Preface: 'neither is it of the least Moment to enquire whether the Colonel hath told his own Story true or not; If he has made it a History or a Parable, it will be equally useful, and capable of doing Good.' It is this aspect which gives the story its fairytale quality, the sense that what is being described is both a realistic account in the vein of his previous narratives and an allegory of man as a social animal. There is more than a hint of the picaresque narrative about it, an awareness that the novel is unified by the personality of its central character but is in essence a series of unconnected episodes. Fielding's *Jonathan Wild* (1743) and Smollett's *Ferdinand* (1753) are later examples of the genre. Jack is a typical picaroon, in the sense that he lives by his wits and encounters men and women from all walks of life in his search for enlightenment.

Defoe's fiction is open to the criticism that the central characters – Crusoe, Moll, Roxana – are vividly rendered but that the secondary characters are less convincingly realised. He normally has a single narrator who is a fully rounded figure surrounded by a gallery of lesser actors who never quite convince us of their reality. To adopt E. M. Forster's famous distinction between 'flat' and 'round' characters, most of his fictional personalities are flat.[55] *Colonel Jack* possesses an interesting exception to this generalisation in Jack's first wife. The account of their courtship and marriage, his gradual disillusionment and his decision to divorce her (pp. 186–98) is one of the finest sequences in the novel and further evidence of Defoe's increasing mastery in depicting human relationships. Throughout the description of their conversations and their life together one has the inescapable awareness of a real person with all that that implies in emotional terms. Despite her profligacy and deceit Jack cares deeply for her; the final moment of parting is moving in its intensity:

> It is true, and I must acknowledge it, that all this was a very Melancholy Scene of Life to me, and but that she took Care by carrying her self to the last Degree Provoking, and continually to Insult me, I cou'd never have gone on to the parting, with so much Resolution, for I really lov'd her very sincerely, and could have been any thing but a Beggar, and a Cuckold with her, but those were intollerable to me, especially, as they were put upon me with so much Insult, and Rudeness. (p. 198)

It is interesting to compare this account with similar descriptions in the novels of Wells or Dickens.[56] Particularly effective is the way in which Defoe conveys Jack's mingled feelings of sadness and affection, his determination to sever their relationship, coupled with his knowledge of his love for her. Defoe was one of the earliest novelists in the English language to attempt a description of an unhappy marriage and the emotional traumas involved. It is true that we only have the account from one point of view: it would be interesting to have her version of their relationship, but that is perhaps too much to ask for. Jack's relief when she re-enters his life is unmistakable and their final reconciliation is convincingly handled. In the interim, husband and wife have both matured. Each now recognises the other's true worth and is prepared to make a real effort to make the marriage work.

Much of the interest of the novel lies in its insight into Defoe's preoccupation with economic man:

> I had now, as above, a House, a Stable, two Ware-houses, and 300 Acres of Land; but as we say, bare Walls make giddy Hussy's, so I had neither Axe or Hatchet, to cut down the Trees; Horse, or Hog, or Cow to put upon the Land; not a Hoe, or a Spade to break Ground, nor a Pair of Hands, but my own to go to Work upon it. (p. 152)

In common with his other narrators, Jack is a self-made figure, a case study in economic and social advancement. He shares with Crusoe (and, one infers, with Defoe) a fascination with trade, with the accumulation of wealth and with what may be achieved through diligence and hard work. When, a few paragraphs later, Jack reflects that even 'the most despicable ruined man in the world has here a fair opportunity put into his hands to begin the world again' (p. 153), he is echoing a view his creator expressed many times in his own person and through his fiction: that man is responsible for his own survival and must make the best of his circumstances, however unpromising. Each of the adventures encountered by Jack is a reflection of Defoe's lifelong interest in many aspects of life – crime, trade, travel, piracy, soldiering. From this point of view *Colonel Jack* can be regarded as 'an amalgam of all the genres he had so far tried'.[57] There is the preoccupation with the criminal underworld of London and with the acquisition of money, both previously displayed in *Moll Flanders*. There is the fascination with overseas travel and piracy evidenced in *Captain Singleton*, and the affection for the life of a soldier witnessed by *Memoirs of a Cavalier*. In the account of Jack's military career in Scotland and Italy there is the same awareness of history and social forces which we have previously seen in *A Journal of the Plague Year*. Above all, there is throughout the narrative a focus on man as an economic animal, a creature who must employ all his resources of intelligence and adaptability in order to triumph over his environment.

As always with Defoe, one is struck by the vivid phrase, the simile that illuminates a page by its aptness to life: 'He had much the Nature of a Bull Dog, bold and desperate, but not generous at all' (p. 5); 'I had never stolen any thing in my Life, and if a Goldsmith had left me in his Shop with heaps of Money, strew'd all round me, and bade me look after it, I should not have touch'd it, I was so honest' (p. 19)

What distinguishes *Colonel Jack* from much of the fiction of its time is Defoe's ability to assume the personality and attitudes of his narrator and to identify with him both mentally and emotionally through all the vicissitudes of his life.

There is a delightful episode early in the novel when the young narrator, a budding thief, hides some money in a hollow tree. To his chagrin the money falls inside the trunk where he cannot reach it:

As young as I was, I was now sensible what a Fool I was before, that I could not think of Ways to keep my Money, but I must come thus far to throw it into a Hole where I could not reach it; well, I thrust my Hand quite up to my Elbow, but no Bottom was to be found, or any End of the Hole or Cavity; I got a Stick off of the Tree and thrust it in a great Way, but all was one; then I cry'd, nay I roar'd out, I was in such a Passion, then I got down the Tree again, then up again, and thrust in my Hand again till I scratch'd my Arm and made it bleed, and cry'd all the while most violently: Then I began to think I had not so much as a half Penny of it left for a half Penny Roll, and I was a hungry, and then I cry'd again: Then I came away in despair, crying, and roaring like a little Boy that had been whip'd, then I went back again to the Tree, and up the Tree again, and thus I did several Times. (p. 25)

The episode is strongly reminiscent of *Robinson Crusoe* in its circumstantial detail. The reader identifies with Jack in his frustration ('roaring like a little Boy that had been whip'd'), his annoyance at his own lack of foresight, his self-inflicted wounds. The vividness of the description is greatly enhanced by the use of active language:

'throw', 'thrust', 'cried', 'roared', 'scratched'. Jack does not simply climb the tree once but several times, so reluctant is he to admit defeat. Characteristically it is not so much the thought of his lost wealth which moves him as the reflection that he is hungry and cannot afford to buy food. Engaging too is his admission of his own foolhardiness: 'I was now sensible what a Fool I was'. Like Crusoe, Jack confides his problems to his reader, shares his thoughts and feelings and is not afraid to look foolish in the eyes of his audience.

Though *Colonel Jack* was evidently written at great speed and displays some indications of tiredness, Defoe's sureness of touch as a stylist is such that the reader is carried irresistibly forward in a lively succession of adventures. As an example of Defoe's technique let us take the following encounter between Jack and his master, in which the unscrupulous master is seeking to train the naïve Jack as a thief:

> They paid him the Money in Gold, and he made hast enough in Telling it over, and came away, passing by me, and going into Three-King-Court, on the other Side of the way; then we cross'd back into Clements-Lane, made the best of our way to Cole-Harbour, at the Water-side, and got a Sculler for a Penny to carry us over the Water to St Mary Overs Stairs, where we Landed, and were safe enough.
>
> Here he turns to me Col. Jack, says he, I believe you are a lucky Boy, this is a good Jobb, we'll go away to St George's Fields, and Share our Booty; aways we went to the Fields, and sitting down in the Grass far enough out of the Path, he pull'd out the Money, look here Jack, says he, did you ever see the like before in your Life? no, never says I, and added very innocently, must we have it all? we have it! says he, who should have it? Why says I, must the Man have none of it again that lost it; he have it again! says he, what d'ye mean by that; Nay, I don't know, says I, why you said just now you would let him have the t'other Bill again, that you said was too big for you.
>
> He Laught at me, you are but a little Boy says he, that's true, but I thought you had not been such a Child neither.... (p. 21)

Jack's innocence and Robin's duplicity are well caught in this passage, but the episode has a deeper significance as an illustration of Defoe's skilful use of language. The passage begins in the past tense ('he made hast enough in Telling it over, and came away'), but soon changes to the present ('Here he turns to me', 'says he', 'says I'). The shift in tense strengthens the air of immediacy, as does the proliferation of language suggestive of movement: 'passing by me', 'going into', 'then we crossed back', 'made the best of our way', 'away we went'. The incident as a whole, though minuscule in relation to the broad sweep of Jack's adventures, is an interesting example of Defoe's gift for conveying a sense of activity. The particularity of the description is characteristic of the author: each reference to a location is followed by a phrase adding corroborative detail to the account:

Three-King-Court	on the other Side of the way
Cole-Harbour	at the Water-side
St Mary Overs Stairs	where we Landed, and were safe enough
St George's Fields	far enough out of the Path.

The fact that the ferry costs one penny adds a pleasing touch of circumstanciality. The technique is not simply in the reiteration of place-names; it is in the accumulation of detail to such an extent that scepticism is dispelled. It is a hallmark of Defoe's style that the reader has a powerful sense of reality: *this*, one feels, actually occurred. In writing the first paragraph the narrator sees the landscape clearly in his mind's eye: it is as if a map of London is unfolded before him. The second paragraph reinforces the air of solidity conveyed by the first: 'sitting down in the Grass far enough out of the Path', 'he pull'd out the Money', 'he Laugh at me'.

Not the least of the reasons why *Colonel Jack* has risen in critical esteem is that it contains clear evidence of Defoe's increasing command of his material – in the handling of dialogue, the depiction of relationships and the presentation of emotion. Though somewhat overshadowed by *Moll Flanders*, it is slowly gaining recognition as a *Bildungsroman* in which Defoe establishes an intimate bond between narrator and reader and depicts a central character who is appealingly lifelike in his gullibility. The fact that Jack learns by his own mistakes does not diminish his achievement. When he remarks at the end of his adventures that 'just Reflections were the utmost Felicity of human life' and that he had not foreseen 'that the Writings of our own Stories would be so much the Fashion in England'(p. 307) he is underlining the didactic element of his story: that in giving an account of his life he has written not only an

A Defoe Companion

entertaining tale but a moral fable. For Jack is indeed a 'truly honourable' man whose nature becomes evident to the reader and to himself as the story proceeds. The revelation is a slow process, for an important subsidiary theme in the novel is that of concealment. The hero spends much of his time on the run or in hiding, living under an assumed name or posing as a man of substance. This life of deception is made explicit in the following passage:

> I had nothing to do now, but entirely to conceal myself, from all that had any knowledge of me before, and this was the easiest thing in the World to do; for I was grown out of every Body's knowledge, and most of those I had known were grown out of mine.... (p. 184)

The concealment is not simply a matter of deluding others as to his identity but deluding himself as to his true nature. Throughout his career as a pickpocket he is uncomfortably aware that he is violating his innermost self, despite his attempts to shout down his better judgement: 'I had no Sense of Conscience, no Reproaches upon my Mind for having done amiss' (p. 60). This denial is followed by repeated assertions of his guilt, passages which abound in such expressions as 'abhorrence', 'cruelty', 'distaste', 'justice', 'villainy', 'abominable', 'wicked', 'repent'. Through all his adventures Jack is not only gaining in maturity, in the sense that he enhances his self – confidence and sheds naïveté, but he loses his illusions concerning himself. Far from being a man without standards, he is upright and moral, a gentleman in the fullest sense. Far from being a coward, he has proved that he is a person of mettle. Far from being indifferent to his former wife, he is a man of compassion deeply concerned for her welfare. In his own words: 'Men never know themselves till they are tried, and Courage is acquired by time, and Experience of things' (p. 208). *Colonel Jack* has never acquired the popularity of *Robinson Crusoe* or *Moll Flanders* but it merits a place in the history of the novel as a valiant attempt to present an honourable protagonist who triumphs over many obstacles to become master of his fate.

Roxana

To read Defoe's fiction in the order in which it was written is to witness an unmistakable development in the craft of the novel. Each brings the genre a step nearer to the art form we are familiar with today, until at last with *Roxana* (1724) we arrive at a complete full-dress novel that is recognisably a precursor of the fiction of Dickens and Hardy. Technically it is a more sophisticated novel than its predecessors, making extensive use of flashback and possessing a symmetrical structure unusual in Defoe's work. Though superficially *Roxana* and *Moll Flanders* have much in common – both are autobiographical narratives purportedly written by women, and both portray a central character who rises to material prosperity through a career of deception – Roxana is a far more complex character than Moll. What makes *Roxana* the more satisfying and profound novel of the two is, first, the depth of the heroine's inner life and, secondly, Defoe's skill in creating a study in moral disintegration.

Roxana is seen both from the inside and the outside. At the outset of her narrative she warns her readers that her account will be presented with detachment:

> Being to give my own Character, I must be excused to give it as impartially as possible, and as if I was speaking of another body: and the Sequel will lead you to judge whether I flatter myself or no. (p. 6)

What enables the reader to view her from both an inner and an outer perspective – to see her 'in the round' – is that many of the central episodes of the novel are described not only in relation to Roxana herself but to her faithful maid Amy. From a comparatively minor character, Amy gradually becomes a figure of crucial importance, complementing her mistress through the vicissitudes of her life and acting as counsel, ally and confidante.

The nature of the two women is such that Amy's instinctive, emotional qualities balance Roxana's more rational and calculating temperament. Where Amy is passionate, Roxana is conventional and introspective; where Amy is impulsive Roxana is cautious. The relationship between the two is developed with considerable effectiveness, the maid becoming indispensable to her mistress through her devotion and reliability. Each possesses qualities admired by the other. An interesting example of this relationship is their conversation prior to Roxana's seduction by her landlord. Roxana is determined to resist the man's overtures; her maid urges her to succumb. The result is a conversation (pp. 39–40) in which each reveal aspects of their temperament that are constant throughout the story and in which each attempts to convince the other of her greater wisdom. The dialogue is worth close study as an example of an exchange between two women who are both convinced of their rightness and reluctant to concede the validity of the other's arguments. At last Roxana sums up the conversation with the words: 'Thus Amy and I canvassed the Business between us; the Jade prompted the Crime, which I had but too much Inclination to commit' (p. 40). Her natural inclination is towards caution but she has to admit that Amy, while erring on the side of impetuosity, is the greater realist of the two.

Throughout Roxana's career as a courtesan and woman of the world Amy remains loyal to her, sharing in her moral decline and assisting her in all her exploits. But whereas Roxana becomes visibly hardened by her life of avarice, Amy remains in essence a woman of simple feelings and is aware of the double standard of her mistress's career. During a terrible storm at sea Amy is frightened into repentance for her immoral life. Her conviction that she will be drowned and go to hell for her misdeeds forces Roxana into compassion for her:

> it immediately occur'd to me, Poor Amy! what art thou, that I am not? what hast thou been, that I have not been? Nay, I am guilty of my own Sin, and thine too: Then it came to my Remembrance, that I had not only been the same with Amy, but that I had been the Devil's Instrument, to make her wicked; that I had a stripp'd her, and prostituted her to the very Man that I had been Naught with myself; that she had but follow'd me; I had been her wicked Example; and I had led her into all; and that as we had sinn'd together, now we were likely to sink together.
>
> (pp. 125–6)

The key phrase here is surely: 'Poor Amy! what art thou, that I am not? what hast thou been, that I have not been? Nay, I am guilty of my own Sin, and thine too.' This acknowledgement of a direct bond between the two characters – that Roxana is responsible for her maid's degeneration as well as her own – underlines one of the dominant themes of the novel: that Amy is a surrogate figure, a second self corresponding to the darker, irrational aspects of Roxana's psyche.[58] Roxana is frequently a deeply divided person, torn between loyalty to those close to her and her pursuit of material prosperity. An instance of this duality is when she is torn between feelings of loyalty to the merchant who has always been a good friend to her and her aspiration to be a princess. The struggle in her conscience between obligation and ambition forms a revealing contrast:

> During this time, I had a strange Elevation upon my Mind; and the Prince or the Spirit of him, had such a Possession of me, that I spent most of this Time in the reallizing all the Great Things of a Life with the Prince, to my Mind; pleasing my Fancy with the Grandeur I was supposing myself to enjoy; and withal, wickedly studying in what Manner to put off this Gentleman, and be-rid of him for-ever.
>
> I cannot but say, that sometimes the Baseness of the Action stuck hard with me; the Honour and Sincerity with which he had always treated me; and, above all, the Fidelity he had shew'd me at Paris, and that I ow'd my Life to him; I say, all these star'd in my Face; and I frequently argued with myself upon the Obligation I was under, to him; and how base wou'd it be, now too, after so many Obligations and Engagements, to cast him off?
>
> But the Title of Highness, and of a Princess, and all those fine things, as they came in, weigh'd down all this; and the Senće of Gratitude vanish'd, as if it had been a Shadow. (pp. 234–5)

She is perfectly open in her self-recrimination: she describes her behaviour as 'wicked' and 'base' and freely admits that, despite the merchant's fidelity towards her, when weighed against the prince's wealth her sense of gratitude vanished 'as if it had been a Shadow'. The use of the word 'shadow' here is suggestive and reinforces our sense of the novel as a psychological study. Throughout the novel there is a duality between rational and irrational, compassion and selfishness, moral and immoral. Roxana has material prosperity yet is deeply unhappy. She has economic security yet is torn by self-doubt. The divided self is evident at many points in her story, as when she meets again the Dutch merchant who had courted her in years past but cannot make up her mind whether to acknowledge him or not. She describes her thoughts as 'Thus fluctuating, and unconcluding . . . what I so earnestly desired, I declined when it offered itself . . . In short, my Thoughts were all confused, and in the utmost Disorder' (p. 222). The episode typifies her indecision at moments of crisis; as always, she is torn between her better and her worse self, between humanity and selfishness.

Again and again Roxana confesses her true nature, as when she remarks apropos of one of her suitors: 'I confess, when he said this, it made all the Blood turn in my Veins, and I thought I should have fainted; poor Gentleman! thought I, you know little of me; what would I give to be really what you think of me!' (p. 137). Or again when rejecting an offer of marriage from an honourable man, she confides to the reader:

> If ever any Man in the World was truly valuable for the strictest honesty of Intention, this was the Man; and if ever Woman in her Senses rejected a Man of Merit, on so trivial and frivolous a Pretence, I was the Woman; but surely it was the most preposterous thing that ever Woman did.   (p. 157)

Most striking of all is a passage in which she contrasts her own selfishness and duplicity against the goodness of her husband: 'His was all Tenderness, all Kindness, and the utmost Sincerity; Mine all Grimace and Deceit; a Piece of meer Manage, and framed Conduct, to conceal a past Life of Wickedness' (p. 300). In these and other passages Roxana draws attention to the fundamental flaw in her nature: that the whole pattern of her life is based on deceit. Time and again she adopts a disguise or an assumed name in order to avoid exposure: the narrative is peppered with such terms as 'disguise', 'counterfeit', 'concealed', 'cheat', 'discovery', 'pretence'. It is significant that when accepting an offer of marriage she describes the new phase in her circumstances as putting an end 'to all the intriguing Part of my Life; a Life full of prosperous Wickedness' (p. 243), although even then she is still plotting to continue a life of duplicity.

One of the many reasons why *Roxana* is such a fascinating work is that the heroine is fully aware of the dichotomy in her own nature and of her deviousness. It is not that the reader is aware of her duplicity while she herself is not; on the contrary, she seems fully cognisant of the defects in her temperament and confesses them frankly in telling her story. Her conversational manner of narration and intimate relationship with the reader heightens the effect of a confessional. It is as if she is dissecting her innermost self, letting us see that for all her outward calm she is a tormented soul within, torn between humane and ignoble motives.

In the final sequence of the novel (p. 276 onwards) when, to her chagrin, Roxana encounters her daughter Susan, there is a powerful sense of retribution closing in on the heroine. Roxana has no wish to be reminded of her misspent past, nor does she want her husband to know she has a daughter by a previous marriage. The atmosphere of impending catastrophe is heightened by such phrases as 'And I am not come to the worst of it yet'; 'I was now under a new Perplexity'; 'I was knocked down again as with a Thunder-Clap'; 'But I was not at the End of my Mortifications yet'. The closing scenes, in which Roxana cries out to the reader that 'I was continually perplexed with this Hussy, and thought she haunted me like an Evil Spirit' (p. 310), possess the intensity of a novel by Hardy or George Eliot. In being compelled to choose between acknowledging her own daughter or rejecting her, Roxana is faced with a crisis of decision: whether to accept Susan (and thus embrace the compassionate side of her nature, her feelings of affection and humanity) or shun her (and thus retain her comfortable life of wealth and respectability). By choosing the latter course she condemns herself to unending reproach, for she knows she has rejected her better self. That Roxana is fully aware of the enormity of her actions and of the correlation between Susan and her wiser self is clear from the following passage:

> As for the poor Girl herself, she was ever before my Eyes; I saw her by Night, and by Day; she haunted my imagination, if she did not haunt the House; my Fancy showed her me in a hundred Shapes and Postures; sleeping or waking, she was with me . . . the Girl was the very Counterpart of myself. (pp. 325, 329)

The language inevitably suggests a double, a self inseparably linked with oneself. One is reminded of William Wilson in Poe's short story: a *doppelgänger* who haunts the narrator to the point of unendurability.[59] The girl, declares Roxana, 'hunted me, as if, like a Hound, she had had a hot Scent' (p. 317). Roxana attempts to flee from her pursuer and adopts a pseudonym, but in vain. Her daughter clings to her with the tenacity of a sleuth. Finally Roxana becomes a prisoner in her own house, unable to emerge for fear of recognition. In her anxiety to avoid detection she becomes a virtual recluse.

Thus her quest for material well-being has come full circle. Her progression from poverty to riches has involved a steady enlargement of her horizons – measured in terms of grand houses, elaborate meals, costly jewels and titled friends. But in the end she is reduced to confinement, a victim of her own selfishness. Her life has closed in on her, bringing neither happiness nor freedom. Contentment is as far away from her as ever, for in the closing pages of the novel she is 'perplexed' and 'troubled', haunted by her love for Susan and the knowledge that, in spurning her, she has violated her own instincts.

Much critical discussion has focused on the novel's abrupt ending. *Roxana* is unusual in that it simply peters out. We are never told explicitly that Susan has been murdered by Amy, nor are we given any detail of Roxana's or Amy's subsequent life. There is merely a brief final paragraph declaring that Roxana 'fell into a dreadful Course of Calamities, and Amy also', and that 'the Blast of Heaven seemed to follow the Injury done the poor Girl, by us both'. The truth seems to be that, having decided on a tragic ending for the novel, the first-person narration presented Defoe with insoluble technical problems. He found himself unable to follow through to a sustained conclusion the tragic climax on which he had embarked, for this would involve the heroine describing in detail her own moral destruction. He contented himself with hinting at it rather than presenting a step-by-step account of the denouement: hence the apparently truncated ending. Even as it is, it remains a powerful piece of writing, unique in Defoe's fiction in that it mounts to an oppressive sense of catastrophe which seems to round off Roxana's career of selfishness.

The sense that Roxana is moving towards a tragic fate is presaged by a sentence in which she confesses her inner torment:

> And let nobody conclude from the strange Success I met with in all my wicked Doings, and the vast Estate which I had raised by it, that therefore I either was happy or easie: No, no, there was a Dart struck into the Liver; there was a secret Hell within, even all the while, when our Joy was at the highest. (p. 260)

This 'secret hell within' – her knowledge of her own unscrupulous past – finally overwhelms her in a vortex of terror. When Amy offers to murder Susan in order to rid her mistress of her tormentor and free her from her past, this is to Roxana the ultimate calamity, bringing the story to an abrupt and horrifying end.

Haunting and terrible as it is, the closing sequence possesses a unity rarely found in Defoe's fiction. Moreover, it gives a shape to the novel as a whole. Whereas *Moll Flanders* and *Colonel Jack* are comparatively shapeless narratives, *Roxana* is much more consciously 'written'. It possesses a thematic unity the earlier fictions lack, a sense of logical design.[60] In place of the loose, episodic structure of *Moll Flanders* there is a sense of moving towards a resolution, a moment of finality.

Defoe could, after all, have opted for a conventional happy ending – as he had done in *Moll Flanders* and *Colonel Jack*. But this would seem all wrong, given what has gone before. In contrast to the unpredictability of the earlier narratives *Roxana* is pervaded by a sense of judgement closing in on the heroine: her fate is determined by her character. A conventional ending in which Roxana subsides into domestic happiness, absolved of her past sins, clearly violated Defoe's instincts as a novelist – however tempted he may have been to round off the story in this way.

For all these reasons *Roxana* is much closer to a true novel than are *Captain Singleton* or *Colonel Jack* because it deals with human relationships in a much fuller and more complex way. The relationships between Roxana and Amy and between Roxana and the merchant (whom she eventually marries) are handled with a maturity and assurance Defoe rarely equalled. These are balanced by the tension between the heroine and her daughter, foredoomed like the others to end in tragedy. Underlying the pattern of relationships sustaining the novel is a series of motifs reinforcing the structure of opposites on which it is based:

emotional	rational
duty	ambition
compassion	selfishness
candour	deceit
freedom	confinement

What so impresses the reader after the complacency of some of the earlier narratives is the sombre mood of *Roxana*. It is a much darker novel than *Moll Flanders* or *Colonel Jack*, more introspective, more riven with self-doubt. There is a sense of foreboding that is lacking in the earlier novels, an awareness that the heroine is increasingly overwhelmed by feelings of guilt and recrimination. Throughout the story she is attempting to escape from her past by adopting a series of disguises and pretences. At the end her past catches up with her: she is finally overcome by her sense of guilt, her awareness of the inconsistencies in her life and of the inexorable link between her actions and the consequences. In this context the novel is a tragedy and Roxana is a tragic heroine who merits a place in literary history alongside Hardy's tormented females. Utterly lacking in the self-satisfaction of Moll or Jack, she is a terrible object-lesson in corruption, in the insidious way in which greed can overcome man's finer motives.

Throughout the narrative one is aware of Roxana's point of view as the narrator telling the story of her life, and of Defoe's point of view as the novelist shaping the story into a literary form. His attitude towards his heroine is ambivalent, for it is never entirely clear whether he sympathises with her or not. Clearly, he is fascinated by her career as a courtesan and woman of fortune but repelled by her amorality: he cannot conceal his distaste that inwardly she is 'a She-Devil, whose whole Conversation for twenty five years had been black as Hell' (p. 301). A clue to his attitude towards her is the passage in which she offers her story as a case study in moral corruption:

> Thus blinded by my own Vanity, I threw away the only Opportunity I then had, to have effectually settl'd my Fortunes, and secur'd them for this World; and I am a Memorial to all that shall read my Story; a standing Monument of the Madness and Distraction which Pride and Infatuations from Hell runs us into; how ill our Passions guide us; and how dangerously we act, when we follow the Dictates of an ambitious Mind.
>
> (p. 161)

'I am a Memorial to all that shall read my Story', she declares. A persuasive reading of the novel, then, is to regard it as a study in degeneration, as an object lesson in self-delusion. Roxana is surely one of the supreme examples in English literature of a heroine who is corrupted by her own vanity and who, by rejecting the promptings of conscience, becomes a victim of her self-centredness. In inviting the reader to judge her, Defoe presents us with a fascinating study of human nature and a classical example of the divided self.

A Tour through the Whole Island of Great Britain

Defoe's *Tour through the Whole Island of Great Britain* was published in three volumes between 1724 and 1726. It is written in the form of a series of letters, each describing a circuit or journey 'giving a particular and diverting account of whatever is curious and worth observation... particularly fitted for the reading of such as desire to travel over the island'. It purports to be a guidebook or conducted tour of England, Wales and Scotland based on a series of journeys undertaken on horseback by Defoe between 1722 and 1724 but, in common with *A Journal of the Plague Year*, it is not quite what it seems to be. Like Sterne's *A Sentimental Journey* and Orwell's *The Road to Wigan Pier*, it is a literary re-creation, a distillation of thoughts and impressions gleaned over a considerable period of time. As merchant, soldier, secret agent and journalist he had travelled widely through Britain over a period of 35 years, 1685–1720. His sharp observation, coupled with his wide reading, his knowledge of political and commercial matters and gift for reportage meant that he was uniquely qualified to present a general picture of Britain at a time of social and economic transition. Pat Rogers has observed that the *Tour* offers 'the densest mixture of history and prophecy, myth and reportage, observation and impression, formal coverage and informal anecdote'.[61] Given Defoe's eclectic background and wide accumulation of curious lore, it is hardly surprising that the book contains a wonderfully detailed portrait of the country written by a man who has little interest in sightseeing in the conventional sense but a shrewd insight into human nature and the English temperament. As he himself defined his aims: 'I have nothing to do with the longtitude of places, the antiquities of towns, corporations, buildings, charters, & c., but to give you a view of the whole in its present state, as also of the commerce, curiosities and customs, according to my title' (p. 480).

Much of the fascination of the *Tour* lies in the fact that Defoe's account is one of the few contemporary portraits of Britain before the Industrial Revolution. Because he presents an overview of the nation during the closing years of the seventeenth century and the opening of the eighteenth it might he supposed that his picture is of a pastoral idyll, a land unchanged and unchanging. His picture is the antithesis of this. What we see most vividly brought to life is an evocation of a country in transition, a landscape concerned not only with agriculture but with manufacturing and trade, with the rise of the mercantile age. For though Defoe is writing before the coming of steam and machinery, there is already evident in his account the rise of a powerful middle class, the emergence of cities and suburbs, a growing preoccupation with wealth and commerce, and the beginnings of productive industry. The landscape described in the *Tour* is by no means a static one but one on the eve of far-reaching transformation and already containing the seeds of the modern age. Whilst London was then, as now, the principal city in the land (its population was then about 700,000), towns such as Birmingham, Manchester and Liverpool were growing in importance as centres of trade and population. Defoe was keenly aware of the significance of transport and commerce, farming and rural life, crafts, ports and roads. His overview of Britain on the eve of the change from the domestic system to the factory system offers an informative, idiosyncratic guide to the nation and its people.

At times the book appears to ramble, partly because of his tendency to digress and partly because he cannot resist passing on any information to the reader he finds interesting or pertinent. He is also determined to cover the ground thoroughly, even if this means returning to places he has already visited: 'yet I may take a review of some parts as I come back, and so may be allowed to pick up any fragments I may have left behind in my going out' (p. 455). Though the *Tour* is undoubtedly discursive, it is a far more logically organised book than its rambling manner may suggest. It is divided into thirteen chapters or 'letters' comprising a thorough exploration of the mainland of Britain, including not only the principal towns but the shire counties and many lesser-known villages and settlements. His love of order can be seen in his frequent lists and tables: a summary of the principal trades of Somerset; a list of the market towns in Norfolk; the clothing towns in the West Country; the staff of Ripon cathedral; the staff of the Oxford colleges; the goods produced in Scotland, and so on. The English passion for methodicalness, exemplified so richly in Crusoe's penchant for lists and summaries, is evident at every stage of his itinerary. Defoe is resolved to omit no detail which may add to the reader's understanding of a town or county. It is for this reason that the book is so full of information – historical, topographical, economic, ecclesiastic – that he considers relevant to his task. From its pages the reader obtains a three-dimensional panorama of the whole country, its sights, smells, trades and peculiarities. There can be few guide-books which so powerfully convey the essence of a landscape in all its aspects.

The *Tour* is quite different from a Baedeker or a Blue Guide offering a dry, factual introduction to a town or a region. There are many points in the narrative where the reader has a vivid awareness of history unfolding before one's eyes, as in Defoe's eye-witness account of a skirmish between William of Orange's troops and forces loyal to King James (pp. 270–5) or his description of London housing before the Great Fire of 1666:

> The streets were not only narrow, and the houses all built of timber, lath and plaster, or, as they were very properly called paper work. But the manner of the building in those days, one story projecting out beyond another, was such, that in some narrow streets, the houses almost touched one another at the top, and it has been known, that men, in case of fire, have escaped on the tops of the houses, by leaping from one side of a street to another; this made it often, and almost always happen, that if a house was on fire, the opposite house was in more danger to be fired by it, according as the wind stood, than the houses next adjoining on either side. How this has been regulated, how it was before, and how much better it now is, I leave to be judged, by comparing the old unburnt part of the city with the new.   (pp. 296–7)

This has all the vividness of a childhood memory, but whether actually seen with Defoe's eyes or not, it possesses an immediacy altogether lacking in many history books. The description of men escaping by 'leaping from one side of a street to another' remains indelibly in the mind, as does his reminder that in London before the Fire 'the buildings looked as if they had been formed to make one general bonfire, whenever any wicked party of incendiaries think fit' (p. 296).

Wherever one opens the pages the reader senses an individual voice commenting, observing, appraising. Thus, when describing the Pool of London (p. 317) he takes the trouble to *count* the number of ships he sees, and observes on the next page: 'But I must land, lest this part of the account seems to smell of the tar.' Always his concern is with practicalities, with the details of organisation, method and trade which generate the nation's livelihood. Witness his careful summary of London's buildings (pp. 321–2) or his famous description of cloth manufacture in the West Riding of Yorkshire (pp. 491–503). At the same time his preoccupation with the here and now is balanced by a sense of history rooted firmly in his discursive reading and wide knowledge of men and affairs. In his description of ancient roads such as the Fosse Way and Watling Street he observes that 'one cannot help realising those times to the imagination; and though I avoid meddling with antiquity as much as possible in this work, yet in this case a circuit or tour through England would be very imperfect, if I should take no notice of these ways' (p. 406). Nor is his survey lacking in humour. Beneath the sharp intelligence and the eye for detail is a dry sense of humour, sometimes at his own expense. Thus, after describing a journey by ferry across the Humber he observes: 'whether I was sea-sick or not, is not worth notice, but that we were all sick of the passage, any one may suppose' (p. 413); and after an account of the cellars in Nottingham well-stocked with ale he adds: 'nor are they uncommunicative in bestowing it among their friends, as some in our company experienced to a degree not fit to be made matter of history' (p. 452).

A particularly interesting example of his technique is his description of a poor family living in a cave near Wirksworth, Derbyshire:

> There was a large hollow cave, which the poor people by two curtains hanged cross, had parted into three rooms. On one side was the chimney, and the man, or perhaps his father, being miners, had found means to work a shaft or funnel through the rock to carry the smoke out at the top, where the giant's tombstone was. The habitation was poor, 'tis true, but things within did not look so like misery as I expected. Every thing was clean and neat, though mean and ordinary. There were shelves with earthen ware, and some pewter and brass. There was, which I observed in particular, a whole flitch or side of bacon hanging up in the chimney, and by it a good piece of another. There was a sow and pigs running about at the door, and a little lean cow feeding upon a green place just before the door, and the little enclosed piece of ground I mentioned, was growing with good barley; it being then near harvest.

To find out whence this appearance of substance came, I asked the poor woman, what trade her husband was? She said, he worked in the lead mines. I asked her, how much he could earn a day there? she said, if he had good luck he could earn about five pence a day, but that he worked by the dish (which was a term of art I did not understand, but supposed, as I afterwards understood it was, by the great, in proportion to the ore, which they measure in a wooden bowl, which they call a dish). Then I asked, what she did, she said, when she was able to work she washed the ore. But, looking down on her children, and shaking her head, she intimated, that they found her so much business she could do but little, which I easily granted must be true. But what can you get at washing the ore, said I, when you can work? She said, if she worked hard she could gain three-pence a day. (pp. 463–4)

The approach anticipates that of Orwell in *The Road to Wigan Pier* and *Down and Out in Paris and London*: what interests Defoe is the nature of the husband's occupation, how much he earns in a day, and how the family makes ends meet. But his interest does not end here. He is fascinated by surface details: how the smoke escapes through the roof of the cave, what the family have to eat, what furnishings they have, whether the room is clean. It is characteristic of him that the cow kept outside the cave is not simply a cow but 'a little lean cow', whilst the 'little enclosed piece of ground ... growing with good barley' reads like an echo from *Robinson Crusoe*. Another typical detail is 'it being then near harvest'; many writers would have omitted this, but Defoe, with his acute awareness of times and seasons, felt it necessary to include it. 'Every thing was clean and neat, though mean and ordinary' is a phrase that could only come from a writer with a novelist's eye for detail. One recalls the descriptions of rooms in the novels of Dickens and Wells: there is the same sense of acute observation, the same curiosity regarding human behaviour, the same eye for small but telling features. The overall impression is of a camera roving over a room or a dwelling, omitting no particular of concern to the reader and eager to communicate an accurate picture of the whole.

The description of the woman and the cave is followed by a graphic portrayal of a lead miner emerging from an underground shaft:

For his person, he was lean as a skeleton, pale as a dead corpse, his hair and beard a deep black, his flesh lank, and, as we thought, something of the colour of the lead itself, and being very tall and very lean he looked, or we that saw him ascend *ab inferis*, fancied he looked like an inhabitant of the dark regions below, and who was just ascended into the world of light.

Besides his basket of tools, he brought up with him about three quarters of a hundred weight of ore, which we wondered at, for the man had no small load to bring, considering the manner of his coming up; and this indeed make him come heaving and struggling up, as I said at first, as if he had great difficulty to get out; whereas it was indeed the weight that he brought with him.

If any reader thinks this, and the past relation of the woman and the cave, too low and trifling for this work, they must be told, that I think quite otherwise; and especially considering what a noise is made of wonders in this country, which, I must needs say, have nothing in them curious, but much talked of, more trifling a great deal. (p. 467)

This man, whom Defoe describes as 'pale as a dead corpse' and looking 'like an inhabitant of the dark regions below' remains in the imagination because he is brought so vividly to life. The reader has a powerful sense of a subterranean creature resembling one of the Morlocks in Wells's *The Time Machine*, a man who has 'just ascended into the world of light'. But Defoe is not content to describe the man and leave it at that; he is interested in the ore the miner is carrying on his back, and even tells us how much it weighs. Pointedly he ends his account with the reflection that 'if any reader thinks this, and the past relation of the woman and the cave, too low and trifling for this work, they must be told, that I think quite otherwise'. Here as elsewhere he makes it clear that his primary interest is *people:* how they earn their livelihood, their homes and buildings, their markets and shops, shipping and commerce. The fact that the book is still read today, more than 250 years after its publication, is testimony to his descriptive and imaginative powers and his ability to convey the *feel* of the towns and places he is portraying.

Like Cobbett's *Rural Rides* (1830), Defoe's *Tour* offers the fruits of a fact-finding exploration of town and country written by an acutely observant guide. But Defoe is content to describe what he sees rather than advocate any particular point of view, and his account is shaped by emotional as well as didactic concerns. His description of the poor family living in a cave is followed by the admission that he and his companions felt grave for the rest of the day, and concludes: 'And if it has no effect of that kind upon the reader, the defect must be in my telling the story in a less moving manner than the poor woman told it her self' (p. 465). Defoe was a deeply emotional man concerned with values as well as facts; to him England is a country 'full of wonders' (p. 455). Whether describing churches, trades, ports or rivers, his portrait is animated with *feelings* – for people, for history, for scenery. He poured into the book not only the fruits of a lifetime's reflection on the English temperament and landscape but the craftsmanship gained from writing seven full-length works of imagination. The delight in solitude and industry which animates *Robinson Crusoe* is evident in the narrator's love of gardens, his pleasure in rural scenes, his fascination with trades and occupations. The preoccupation with history which brings *Memoirs of a Cavalier* so vividly to life breathes through his descriptions of battles and castles, churches and garrisons. The journalistic skill which distinguishes *A Journal of the Plague Year* is evident on every page in his quest for impartiality, his gift for presenting pen pictures of towns and country seats, his careful listing of background information. Above all, the *Tour* is the work of a man possessing intellectual curiosity and wide knowledge derived from extensive reading, travel and experience.

When reading Defoe one is frequently struck by the fusion of the literal and the imaginative. In common with *The Complete English Tradesman*, the factual content of the *Tour* is richly interspersed with sentences and whole paragraphs bordering on the novelistic, passages which come to life through his gift of description. His account of a journey from Rochdale to Halifax during a snowstorm would not be out of place in *Colonel Jack* or *Captain Singleton*:

> It is not easy to express the consternation we were in when we came up near the top of the mountain; the wind blew exceeding hard and blew the snow directly in our faces, and that so thick, that it was impossible to keep our eyes open to see our way. The ground also was so covered with snow, that we could see no track, or when we were in the way, or when out; except when we were showed it by a frightful precipice on one hand, and uneven ground on the other; even our horses discovered their uneasiness

at it; and a poor spaniel dog that was my fellow traveller, and usually diverted us with giving us a mark for our gun, turned tail to it and cried. (pp. 487–8)

What lifts such passages above the commonplace are the vivid turns of phrase that remain in the mind: 'the wind blew the snow directly in our faces'; 'it was impossible to keep our eyes open to see our way'; and the contrast between the 'frightful precipice' on one side and the 'uneven ground' on the other. 'Even our horses discovered their uneasiness at it', he adds, whilst the spaniel who 'turned tail to it and cried' is a touch worthy of the author of *Robinson Crusoe*. Characteristically Defoe describes the dog as 'my fellow traveller' and adds the detail that he 'usually diverted us with giving us a mark for our gun'. This skilfully establishes a bond between man and dog, strongly reminiscent of Crusoe on his island. Today the road from Rochdale to Halifax over Blackstone Edge is a modern motor road, but during winter or at night it remains as wild and inhospitable as he describes it and it is by no means difficult to imagine his plight.

In his Preface Defoe claimed that 'the preparations for this work have been suitable to the author's earnest concern for its usefulness ... in all which the author has not been wanting to treasure up just remarks upon particular places and things' (p. 45). The latter phrase is an apt description of his method, for it is precisely as a compendium of 'just remarks upon particular places and things' that the *Tour* is most read and studied today. G. D. H. Cole asserted that it is 'by far the most graphic contemporary account of the state of economic and social affairs near the beginning of the eighteenth century'.[62] In its breadth of vision, its grasp of detail, its concern with the lives and occupations of ordinary people, it is a remarkable amalgam of Defoe's strengths as a writer. He defined his aim in writing the *Tour* as a resolve 'to have a perfect knowledge of the most remarkable things' (p. 485). It remains essential reading for all who seek a deeper understanding of England before the coming of machinery and who gain enrichment by seeing the landscape through the eyes of a novelist.

Appendix

1. FILM VERSIONS

Numerous film adaptations have been made of Defoe's novels. By common consent the most successful has been the 1953 version of *Robinson Crusoe*, directed by Luis Buñuel. Gavin Lambert described this as 'A film of which the purity, the tense poetic style evokes a kind of wonder'.

The following is a list of the principal film adaptations based on Defoe's stories.

1953   *The Adventures of Robinson Crusoe*
Pathecolor. 89 minutes. Written and directed by Luis Buñuel. Starring Dan O'Herlihy as Crusoe and James Fernandez as Friday. An absorbing version of the famous story, remarkably true to the original.

1964   *Robinson Crusoe on Mars*
Paramount. 110 minutes. Written by Ib Melchoir and John C. Higgins. Starring Paul Mantee and Adam West. Defoe's tale is transplanted to Mars, but the basic shape of the story remains the same. Filmed in Death valley.

1965   *The Amorous Adventures of Moll Flanders*
Paramount. 125 minutes. Written by Dennis Cannan and Roland Kibbee. Directed by Terence Young. Starring Kim Novak as Moll Flanders. Also featured Richard Johnson, George Sanders, Lilli Palmer, Angela Lansbury, Leo McKern and Cecil Parker. A flawed attempt to translate Defoe's novel to the screen in terms of a bawdy romp rather than a psychological study.

1969   *Robinson Crusoe and the Tiger*
Eastmancolor. 110 minutes. Written by Mario Marzac and Rene Cardona Jr. Starring Hugo Stieglitz as Crusoe. An effective version of the novel, with the addition of a tiger which Crusoe adopts as a pet.

2. THE DESERT ISLAND MYTH

Novels inspired by *Robinson Crusoe* are too numerous to itemise in any detail, but the following is a list of the more outstanding stories based in whole or part on Defoe's narrative.

1813   J. R. Wyss, *The Swiss Family Robinson*
The adventures of a Swiss clergyman, his wife and four sons shipwrecked on a desert island.

1857   R. M. Ballantyne, *The Coral Island*
The adventures of three boys shipwrecked on a deserted Pacific island.

1883   R. L. Stevenson, *Treasure Island*
The quest for buried treasure on an island in the West Indies. The character of Ben Gunn, marooned on the island, is based in part on Crusoe.

1896   H. G. Wells, *The Island of Doctor Moreau*
The story of a vivisectionist who carries out experiments on a lonely island in the Pacific. After the death of Moreau and his assistant, the narrator is the only human being left on the island.

1928   S. Fowler Wright, *The Island of Captain Sparrow*
The adventures of a castaway on a remote Pacific island.

1954   William Golding, *Lord of the Flies*
The adventures of a group of schoolboys whose plane crashes on a desert island.

1967   Michael Tournier, *Friday or the Other Island*
A reworking of Defoe's story, in which a young man, the sole survivor of a shipwreck, is washed ashore on a Pacific island.

1986   J. M. Coetzee, *Foe*
Another reworking of the myth, set in 1720. A woman, Susan Barton, approaches Defoe and tells him the story of her adventures on an unknown island.

References

1. Peter Laslett, *The World We Have Lost* (Methuen, London, 1965) p. 80.
2. In *The Protestant Monastery*, written in the autumn of 1726, Defoe described himself as being in his sixty-seventh year.
3. *Review*, 14 February 1713.
4. *Review*, vol. 3, 3 January 1706, p. 7.
5. H. G. Wells, *Tono-Bungay* (Macmillan, London, 1909) Book 2, ch. 1, 1.
6. Daniel Defoe, *The Complete English Tradesman* (Alan Sutton, Gloucester, 1987) p. 60.
7. *Review*, 11 June 1713.
8. Lionel Stevenson, *The English Novel* (Constable, London, 1960) p. 66.
9. Quoted in James Sutherland, *Defoe* (Methuen, London, 1937) pp. 253–4.
10. Introduction to 1810 edition of Defoe's novels, published by John Ballantyne. Quoted in Pat Rogers (ed.), *Defoe: The Critical Heritage* (Routledge & Kegan Paul, London, 1972) p. 76.
11. Virginia Woolf, *The Common Reader* (Hogarth Press, London, 1933) p. 121.
12. Q. D. Leavis, *Fiction and the Reading Public* (Penguin Books, Harmondsworth, Middx, 1979) p. 93.
13. Rogers, *Defoe*, p. 26.
14. Letter to Wells, 3 March 1911. Quoted in L. Edel and G. N. Ray (eds), *Henry James and H. G. Wells* (Rupert Hart-Davis, London, 1958) p. 128.
15. Ian A. Bell, *Defoe's Fiction* (Croom Helm, London, 1985) p. 67.
16. Woolf , *The Common Reader*.
17. Bell, *Defoe's Fiction*, p. 196.
18. R. L. Stevenson, 'My First Book', *The Idler*, August 1894, pp. 2–11; included as ch. 5 of his *Essays in the Art of Writing* (Chatto & Windus, London, 1905).
19. H. G. Wells, 'The Contemporary Novel', 1911; included as ch. 9 of *An Englishman Looks at the World* (Cassell, London, 1914).
20. Wells, *Tono-Bungay*, Book 1, ch. 1.
21. George Orwell, *The English People* (Collins, London, 1947) p. 39.
22. George Orwell, 'Charles Dickens', 1939; included in *Collected Essays, Journalism and Letters* (Penguin Books, Harmondsworth, Middx, 1970) vol. 1, p. 504.
23. Cf. Peter Conrad, *John Fowles* (Methuen, London, 1982) p. 42: '*The Magus* is a compelling, grandly ingenious and oddly childlike book.'
24. R. L. Stevenson, 'A Gossip on Romance', 1882; included as ch. 15 of *Memories and Portraits* (Chatto & Windus, London, 1887).
25. V. O. Birdsall, *Defoe's Perpetual Seekers* (Bucknell University Press, Lewisburg, Pa, 1985) p. 171.
26. F. Bastian, *Defoe's Early Life* (Macmillan, London, 1981) p. 87.
27. Lionel Stevenson, *The English Novel: A Panorama* (Constable, London, 1960) p. 73.

28. G. H. Maynadier, Introduction to *Daniel Defoe: Novels of Adventure and Piracy* (Dial Press, New York, 1935) p. xiv.
29. E. A. Poe, Review of Hawthorne's *Twice-Told Tales*, *Graham's Magazine*, April 1842.
30. H. G. Wells, 'The Diamond Maker', *Pall Mall Budget*, 16 August 1894, later reprinted in *The Stolen Bacillus and Other Incidents* (Methuen, London, 1895).
31. William Freeman, *The Incredible Defoe* (Herbert Jenkins, London, 1950) p. 176.
32. That it continues to fascinate modern writers may be seen from *Friday, or the Other Island* by Michael Tournier (Collins, London, 1969, and Penguin Books, Harmondsworth, Middx, 1974) and *Foe* by J. M. Coetzee (Secker & Warburg, London, 1986 and Penguin Books, Harmondsworth, Middx, 1987), both reworkings of Defoe's central idea.
33. Walter de la Mare, *Desert Islands* (Faber & Faber, London, 1930) p. 37.
34. Cf. *Robinson Crusoe*, pp. 176–9, and H. G. Wells, *Mr Blettsworthy on Rampole Island* (Benn, London, 1928) pp. 199–201. Both writers use the device of a womb-like cave as a retreat from danger.
35. Ian Watt, *The Rise of the Novel* (Penguin Books, Harmondsworth, Middx, 1983) p. 89.
36. Roger Fowler, *A Dictionary of Modern Critical Terms* (Routledge & Kegan Paul, London, 1973) p. 5.
37. Watt, *Rise of the Novel*, p. 82.
38. Ibid., p. 35.
39. Pat Rogers, Preface to *Robinson Crusoe*, Unwin Critical Library (Allen & Unwin, London, 1979) p. vii.
40. For an account of the debate concerning its authorship, see the Introduction by John Mullan to the World's Classics edition of *Memoirs of a Cavalier* (Oxford University Press, London, 1991) pp. vii–xxvi.
41. James Sutherland, *Daniel Defoe: A Critical Study* (Harvard University Press, Cambridge, Mass., 1971) p. 159.
42. Daniel Defoe, *Captain Singleton*, pp. 65, 73, 101, 82.
43. Cf. especially Stevenson's novel *The Master of Ballantrae*, and his short story 'Markheim', in *The Merry Men, and Other Tales* (Chatto & Windus, London, 1887).
44. Sutherland, *Daniel Defoe: A Critical Study*, p. 146.
45. For a detailed examination of the chronology of *Moll Flanders*, see David Leon Higdon, *Time and English Fiction* (Macmillan, London, 1977) pp. 56–62.
46. Wells, *Tono-Bungay*, Book 1, ch. 1, 8.
47. Watt, *The Rise of the Novel*, pp. 136–7.
48. Sutherland, *Defoe*, p. 246.
49. Henry James to H. G. Wells, 3 March 1911, quoted in L. Edel and G. N. Ray (eds), *Henry James and H. G. Wells* (Hart-Davis, London, 1958) p. 128.
50. Anthony Burgess, Introduction to *A Journal of the Plague Year* (Penguin Books, Harmondsworth, Middx, 1984) p. 7.

51. Cf. David Lodge, 'Tono-Bungay and the Condition of England', in *Language of Fiction* (Routledge & Kegan Paul, London, 1966) pp. 214–42; and Lionel Trilling, 'Little Dorrit', in *Dickens: Modern Judgements*, ed. A. E. Dyson (Aurora, London, 1970) pp. 221–32.

52. Cf. H. G. Wells, *The War of the Worlds*, Book 2, 8: 'Dead London', and his *The War in the Air*, ch. 11: 'The Great Collapse'.

53. Wells, *The War of the Worlds*, Book 1, ch. 16: 'The Exodus from London'.

54. Malcolm Bradbury, *The Social Context of Modern English Literature* (Basil Blackwell, Oxford, 1971) p. xxxii.

55. See E. M. Forster, *Aspects of the Novel* (Penguin Books, Harmondsworth, Middx, 1970) pp. 73–89.

56. Cf. Wells, *Tono-Bungay*, Book 2, ch. 4: 'Marion'; and his *The New Machiavelli*, Book 4, ch. 2: 'The Impossible Position'; and Charles Dickens, *David Copperfield*, ch. xliv: 'Our Housekeeping'.

57. Sutherland, *Daniel Defoe: A Critical Study*, p. 198.

58. Cf. the relationship between the Durie brothers in Stevenson's *The Master of Ballantrae*.

59. E. A. Poe, 'William Wilson' (1839), included in *Tales of Mystery and Imagination*. See also Stevenson's short story 'Markheim', in *The Merry Men, and Other Stories* (Chatto & Windus, London, 1887), for an interesting variant on the idea of a *doppelgänger*.

60. David Leon Higdon, in *Time and English Fiction* (Macmillan, London, 1977) pp. 63–73, discusses the carefully worked out time scheme of *Roxana*.

61. Pat Rogers, Introduction to *A Tour through the Whole Island* (Penguin Books, Harmondsworth, Middx, 1986) p. 29.

62. G. D. H. Cole, Introduction to *A Tour through the Whole Island* (J. M. Dent, London, 1962) p. ix.

Bibliography

THE WORKS OF DEFOE

Individual Works

Robinson Crusoe, edited with an introduction by J. Donald Crowley (Oxford University Press, London, 1972).

Memoirs of a Cavalier, edited by James T. Boulton, introduction by John Mullan (Oxford University Press, London 1991).

Captain Singleton, edited by Shiv K. Kumar, introduction by Penelope Wilson (Oxford University Press, London, 1990).

Moll Flanders, edited with an introduction by G. A. Starr (Oxford University Press, London, 1971).

A Journal of the Plague Year, edited by Louis Landa, introduction by David Roberts (Oxford University Press, London, 1990).

Colonel Jack, edited by Samuel Holt Monk, introduction by David Roberts (Oxford University Press, London, 1989).

Roxana, edited with an introduction by Jane Jack (Oxford University Press, London, 1964).

A Tour through the Whole Island of Great Britain, edited with an introduction and notes by Pat Rogers (Penguin Books, Harmondsworth, Middx, 1986).

Collected Editions

The Versatile Defoe: An Anthology of Uncollected Writings by Daniel Defoe, edited and introduced by Laura Ann Curtis (George Prior, London, 1979).

Selected Writings of Daniel Defoe, edited by James T. Boulton (Cambridge University Press, Cambridge, 1975).

Freebooters and Buccaneers: Novels of Adventure and Piracy, edited and introduced by G. H. Maynadier (Dial Press, New York, 1935).

BIOGRAPHY

Bastian, F., *Defoe's Early Life* (Macmillan, London, 1981).

Freeman, William, *The Incredible De Foe* (Herbert Jenkins, London, 1950).

Moore, John Robert, *Daniel Defoe: Citizen of the Modern World* (University of Chicago Press, Chicago, 1958).

Sutherland, James, *Defoe* (Methuen, London, 1937).

CRITICISM

Bell, Ian A., *Defoe's Fiction* (Croom Helm, London, 1985).

Birdsall, Virginia Ogden, *Defoe's Perpetual Seekers: A Study of the Major Fiction* (Associated University Presses, London and Toronto, 1985).

Boardman, Michael M., *Defoe and the Uses of Narrative* (Rutgers University Press, New Brunswick, 1983).

Curtis, Laura A., *The Elusive Daniel Defoe* (Vision Press, London, and Barnes & Noble, New Jersey, 1984).

Furbank, P. N. and Owens, W. R., *The Canonisation of Daniel Defoe* (Yale University Press, New Haven, 1988).

Novak, Maximillian E., *Realism, Myth and History in Defoe's Fiction* (University of Nebraska Press, Lincoln, 1983).

Rogers, Pat, *Robinson Crusoe*, Unwin Critical Library (Allen & Unwin, London, 1979).

Rogers, Pat (ed.), *Defoe: The Critical Heritage* (Routledge & Kegan Paul, London, 1972).

Sutherland, James, *Daniel Defoe: A Critical Study* (Harvard University Press, Cambridge, Mass., 1971).

LITERARY AND HISTORICAL BACKGROUND

Church, Richard, *The Growth of the English Novel* (Methuen, London, 1951).

Earle, Peter, *The World of Defoe* (Weidenfeld & Nicolson, London, 1976).

Karl, Frederick R., *A Reader's Guide to the Development of the English Novel in the 18th Century* (Thames & Hudson, London, 1975).

Laslett, Peter, *The World We Have Lost* (Methuen, London, 1965).

Novak, Maximillian E., *Eighteenth-Century English Literature* (Macmillan, London, 1983).

Speck, W. A., *Reluctant Revolutionaries: Englishmen and the Revolution of 1688* (Oxford University Press, London, 1989).

Watt, Ian, *The Rise of the Novel: Studies in Defoe, Richardson and Fielding* (Chatto & Windus, London, 1957).

Index